THE TRIAL AND DEATH OF SOCRATES

PLATO

With an introduction by
EMMA WOOLERTON

ARCTURUS

Picture credits: Bridgeman 12, 16, 51; Clipart 10, 21, 22, 40, 48, 55, 58, 123; Corbis 37, 104.

Translation: Benjamin Jowett (1817–93).

Introduction: Emma Woolerton read Classics at the University of Cambridge, from which she graduated with her PhD in 2004. She now teaches Latin and Greek for several of the Colleges of the University.

ARCTURUS

This edition published in 2010 by Arcturus Publishing Limited
26/27 Bickels Yard, 151–153 Bermondsey Street,
London SE1 3HA

ISBN: 978-1-84837-590-1
AD001393EN

Printed in China

CONTENTS

INTRODUCTION

Plato's dialogues are among the best-known and most influential ancient Greek texts to have been handed down to us, and the three that relate to the trial and execution of his teacher Socrates on charges of corrupting the young and introducing new gods are fascinating both as philosophical exposés and historical documents. The *Apology* is Plato's representation of Socrates' defence speech at his trial and response to the judgement passed on him. In *Crito*, Socrates is offered a chance to escape but rejects it, explaining his belief that, as a subject of the State, he must submit to its laws. In *Phaedo*, Socrates is visited by friends in prison and assures them that he is not afraid of death – indeed he welcomes it – setting out his belief in the immortality of the soul before drinking poison and dying.

SOCRATES' LIFE AND THE HISTORICAL BACKGROUND TO HIS TRIAL

Socrates is undeniably one of the central figures in the history of Western philosophy. Before his trial and execution in 399BC, he had lived though a period of Greek history marked by the rise of Athens as an imperial power, and the response of Sparta to this rise; the tension between the two powers eventually culminated in two conflicts, the First and Second Peloponnesian Wars, in 460–445 and 431–404. The second of these wars resulted in Athens' defeat, the dissolution of its empire and the imposition of an oligarchic regime, often referred to as the Thirty Tyrants, or the Thirty. They imposed restrictions on freedoms and rights previously enjoyed by all male citizens, as well as condemning hundreds of citizens to death and exiling thousands more. The Thirty were overthrown in 403, and Athens' previous democracy restored.

Socrates' life, as a citizen of Athens, was of course affected by and tied up in this turbulent history. He served, for example, as a

soldier (according to several of Plato's dialogues) in campaigns before and during the Second Peloponnesian War. During the rule of the Thirty, he was asked to participate in taking a citizen from his home to be executed, but refused to comply. Despite this disobedience, Socrates had taught one of the Thirty (Critias) earlier in life and it is possible that this connection played a part in his trial and execution. He does not come across as an ardent supporter of, or participant in, the restored Athenian democracy, and this too may have contributed to his condemnation. As well as political upheaval, Socrates also lived through a period in which some of the certainties that had hitherto underpinned Greek life were challenged and called into question; he was popularly regarded as being strongly connected to this atmosphere of intellectual challenge.

Socrates himself did not write any philosophical works: our knowledge and understanding of him come rather from the works of his contemporaries. Of these, Aristophanes' comic play, *The Clouds* (produced twenty-five years before Socrates' death) is the least flattering; in it, Socrates is represented as the head of a school that charges money to teach rhetorical trickery and leaves its pupils disrespectful of traditional values. This view of Socrates was perceived by his friends and admirers to be damaging and false; after his trial and execution, works appeared attempting to represent Socrates in a manner which seemed more truthful to his students and followers. The most famous of these works are Plato's dialogues.

PLATO AND THE DIALOGUES

We have very little evidence for Plato's early life: we don't know for certain where or when he was born, though most scholars agree on a date between 429 and 427BC for his birth, and 348 or 347BC for his death. He is known to have been a member of a wealthy and politically active family in Athens; his uncles Charmides and Critias were two of the Thirty Tyrants. His real name was probably Aristocles, with Plato (meaning 'broad') being a nickname for his physique, or possibly his wrestling style.

After Socrates' death in 339BC, Plato left Athens and travelled around Greece and Asia Minor, before returning to found a philosophical school, the Academy. Once more, we have no firm evidence as to when it was founded, but the date is usually agreed to have been around the mid-380s. The most famous student of Plato's Academy is Aristotle.

In total, thirty-five dialogues, along with thirteen letters, have been ascribed to Plato since antiquity. The dialogue form as a medium for philosophy appears to have been Plato's innovation – earlier philosophy had been written in poetry – and he uses it to challenge and develop philosophical ideas through close questioning (the exception to this form amongst his works is the *Apology*, which is largely spoken by Socrates alone). The historical accuracy and foundation of the dialogues is impossible to judge, and we should not suppose that the works are verbatim transcriptions of actual conversations (indeed, in the *Phaedo*, Plato mentions explicitly that he is absent, quashing any notion of him as a stenographer in the corner of the room).

Plato reveals very little of himself in his dialogues. The one thing he does make clear is his position as the devoted pupil of Socrates: in the *Apology*, he is named as one of the young men Socrates could be accused of corrupting (see page 29), as well as being willing to contribute towards the payment of a fine in place of the death penalty (see page 33). He is never an interlocutor in the dialogues, meaning that the philosophical ideas which they put

forward are usually found in the mouth of Socrates. However, as his works progress, it is generally agreed that the ideas found in them are Plato's own developments of the teachings of Socrates, rather than notions that Socrates himself expounded.

Plato's earlier works, including both the *Apology* and the *Crito*, are believed to be the most faithful representations of the historical Socrates and his philosophical ideas, and are often referred to as 'the Socratic dialogues'. The *Phaedo* comes from the phase in his writing when Plato appears to have started putting forward his own philosophical notions, such as his Theory of Forms[1], which Socrates uses as the basis of one of his deathbed arguments.

THE SOCRATIC METHOD

In the second half of the 5th century BC, intellectual debate and inquiry, and a particular group of teachers, became highly prominent in Athens. The Sophists (literally 'wisdom men', 'men engaged in the business of wisdom') purported to teach excellence, and had a reputation for being able to make bad arguments beat good ones; their rhetorical skills appear to have been exceptional. A large proportion of them charged fees for teaching their skills to the public; as well as being a participatory democracy, Athens had a strong legal culture, making the acquisition of rhetorical and argumentative ingenuity highly prized, and highly priced. It is clear both from Aristophanes' *The Clouds*, and from remarks made by Socrates in the *Apology*, that he was associated with the Sophists in the popular imagination.

Plato's Socrates states categorically that he does not accept payment for teaching, a crucial difference between the Sophists and himself. He also has a different set of intellectual aims, including a

---

[1] The idea that there are universal forms of things, existing outside of space and time as we understand them, and that the examples we see in our world are simply imperfect replicas of these perfect, ideal forms – compare a hand-drawn equilateral triangle to the idea of a triangle, in which all angles will be perfect.

keen interest in universal concepts and definitions, and sets about his business via a method of close questioning, which has as a result been named the Socratic Method. This method frequently achieves not so much a concrete definition or statement of knowledge as an understanding of the faults of available definitions, and an admission of ignorance. Socrates' interlocutors often end up having their ideas and definitions proved incorrect, often – in the earlier dialogues – without any alternative idea being posited to replace them. They do, however, now know that their previously held views were flawed, an important step in moving towards true knowledge and understanding.

Socrates' determination to prove his own ignorance to others is demonstrated in the *Apology*. It is by our own standards an unconventional defence speech: Socrates describes his search for men who are wiser than him, before concluding that their lack of self-awareness means that the majority of citizens are in fact rather stupid. Yet this does not lead to contempt for the city's institutions and verdicts; in the *Crito*, Socrates argues for the importance of obedience to the city's laws, thereby refusing to take the opportunity offered to him to escape his execution. In the *Phaedo*, we see this sentence carried out, after lengthy philosophical and mythological debate about the nature of the soul and the afterlife. The three dialogues together give a strong portrait of Socrates' character, as well as examples of his argumentative style, and a view of Plato's development of his ideas. They are an excellent introduction to this brilliant and captivating figure, whose intellectual influence has never waned.

Emma Woolerton

APOLOGY

How you have felt, O men of Athens, at hearing the speeches of my accusers, I cannot tell; but I know that their persuasive words almost made me forget who I was – such was the effect of them; and yet they have hardly spoken a word of truth. But many as their falsehoods were, there was one of them which quite amazed me; – I mean when they told you to be upon your guard, and not to let yourselves be deceived by the force of my eloquence. They ought to have been ashamed of saying this, because they were sure to be detected as soon as I opened my lips and displayed my deficiency; they certainly did appear to be most shameless in saying this, unless by the force of eloquence they mean the force of truth; for then I do indeed admit that I am eloquent. But in how different a way from theirs! Well, as I was saying, they have hardly uttered a word, or not more than a word, of truth; but you shall hear from me the whole truth: not, however, delivered after their manner, in a set oration duly ornamented with words and phrases. No indeed! but I shall use the words and arguments which occur to me at the moment; for I am certain that this is right, and that at my time of life I ought not to be appearing before you, O men of Athens, in the character of a juvenile orator – let no one expect this of me. And I must beg of you to grant me one favour, which is this – If you hear me using the same words in my defence which I have been in the habit of using, and which most of you may have heard in the agora, and at the tables of the money-changers, or anywhere else, I would ask you not to be surprised at this, and not to interrupt me. For I am more than seventy years of age, and this is the first time

that I have ever appeared in a court of law, and I am quite a stranger to the ways of the place; and therefore I would have you regard me as if I were really a stranger, whom you would excuse if he spoke in his native tongue, and after the fashion of his country; – that I think is not an unfair request. Never mind the manner, which may or may not be good; but think only of the justice of my cause, and give heed to that: let the judge decide justly and the speaker speak truly.

And first, I have to reply to the older charges and to my first accusers, and then I will go to the later ones. For I have had many accusers, who accused me of old, and their false charges have continued during many years; and I am more afraid of them than of Anytus and his associates, who are dangerous, too, in their own way. But far more dangerous are these, who began when you were children, and took possession of your minds with their falsehoods, telling of one Socrates, a wise man, who speculated about the heaven above, and searched into the earth beneath, and made the worse appear the better cause. These are the accusers whom I dread; for they are the circulators of this rumour, and their hearers are too apt to fancy that speculators of this sort do not believe in the gods. And they are many, and their charges against me are of

ancient date, and they made them in days when you were impressible – in childhood, or perhaps in youth – and the cause when heard went by default, for there was none to answer. And, hardest of all, their names I do not know and cannot tell; unless in the chance of a comic poet. But the main body of these slanderers who from envy and malice have wrought upon you – and there are some of them who are convinced themselves, and impart their convictions to others – all these, I say, are most difficult to deal with; for I cannot have them up here, and examine them, and therefore I must simply fight with shadows in my own defence, and examine when there is no one who answers. I will ask you then to assume with me, as I was saying, that my opponents are of two kinds – one recent, the other ancient; and I hope that you will see the propriety of my answering the latter first, for these accusations you heard long before the others, and much oftener.

Well, then, I will make my defence, and I will endeavour in the short time which is allowed to do away with this evil opinion of me which you have held for such a long time; and I hope I may succeed, if this be well for you and me, and that my words may find favour with you. But I know that to accomplish this is not easy – I quite see the nature of the task. Let the event be as God wills: in obedience to the law I make my defence.

I will begin at the beginning, and ask what the accusation is which has given rise to this slander of me, and which has encouraged Meletus to proceed against me. What do the slanderers say? They shall be my prosecutors, and I will sum up their words in an affidavit. 'Socrates is an evil-doer, and a curious person, who searches into things under the earth and in heaven, and he makes the worse appear the better cause; and he teaches the aforesaid doctrines to others.' That is the nature of the accusation, and that is what you have seen yourselves in the comedy of Aristophanes; who has introduced a man whom he calls Socrates, going about and saying that he can walk in the air, and talking a deal of nonsense concerning matters of which I do not pretend to know either much

or little – not that I mean to say anything disparaging of anyone who is a student of natural philosophy. I should be very sorry if Meletus could lay that to my charge. But the simple truth is, O Athenians, that I have nothing to do with these studies. Very many of those here present are witnesses to the truth of this, and to them I appeal. Speak then, you who have heard me, and tell your neighbours whether any of you have ever known me hold forth in few words or in many upon matters of this sort… You hear their answer. And from what they say of this you will be able to judge of the truth of the rest.

As little foundation is there for the report that I am a teacher, and take money; that is no more true than the other. Although, if a man is able to teach, I honour him for being paid. There is Gorgias of Leontium, and Prodicus of Ceos, and Hippias of Elis, who go the round of the cities, and are able to persuade the young men to leave their own citizens, by whom they might be taught for nothing, and come to them, whom they not only pay, but are thankful if they may be allowed to pay them. There is actually a Parian philosopher residing in Athens, of whom I have heard; and I came to hear of him in this way: I met a man who has spent a world of money on the Sophists, Callias the son of Hipponicus, and knowing that he had sons, I asked him: 'Callias,' I said, 'if your two sons were foals or calves, there would be no difficulty in finding someone to put over them; we should hire a trainer of horses or a farmer probably who would improve and perfect them in their own proper virtue and excellence; but as they are human beings, whom are you thinking of placing over them? Is there anyone who understands human and political virtue? You must have thought about this as you have sons; is there anyone?' 'There is,' he said.

'Who is he?' said I, 'and of what country? and what does he charge?' 'Evenus the Parian,' he replied; 'he is the man, and his charge is five minae.' Happy is Evenus, I said to myself, if he really has this wisdom, and teaches at such a modest charge. Had I the same, I should have been very proud and conceited; but the truth is that I have no knowledge of the kind.

I dare say, Athenians, that someone among you will reply, 'Yes, Socrates, but what is the origin of these accusations which are brought against you; there must have been something strange which you have been doing? All this great fame and talk about you would never have arisen if you had been like other men: tell us, then, why this is, as we should be sorry to judge hastily of you.' Now I regard this as a fair challenge, and I will endeavour to explain to you the origin of this name of 'wise,' and of this evil fame. Please to attend then. And although some of you may think that I am joking, I declare that I will tell you the entire truth. Men of Athens, this reputation of mine has come of a certain sort of wisdom which I possess. If you ask me what kind of wisdom, I reply, such wisdom as is attainable by man, for to that extent I am inclined to believe that I am wise; whereas the persons of whom I was speaking have a superhuman wisdom, which I may fail to describe, because I have it not myself; and he who says that I have, speaks falsely, and is taking away my character. And here, O men of Athens, I must beg you not to interrupt me, even if I seem to say something extravagant. For the word which I will speak is not mine. I will refer you to a witness who is worthy of credit, and will tell you about my wisdom – whether I have any, and of what sort – and that witness shall be the god of Delphi. You must have known Chaerephon; he was early a friend of mine, and also a friend of yours, for he shared in the exile of the people, and returned with you. Well, Chaerephon, as you know, was very impetuous in all his doings, and he went to Delphi and boldly asked the oracle to tell him whether – as I was saying, I must beg you not to interrupt – he asked the oracle to tell him whether there was anyone wiser than I was, and the Pythian prophetess answered that there was no man wiser. Chaerephon is dead himself, but his brother, who is in court, will confirm the truth of this story.

Why do I mention this? Because I am going to explain to you why I have such an evil name. When I heard the answer, I said to myself, What can the god mean? and what is the interpretation of this riddle? for I know that I have no wisdom, small or great. What can he mean when he says that I am the wisest of men? And yet he is a god and cannot lie; that would be against his nature. After a long consideration, I at last thought of a method of trying the question. I reflected that if I could only find a man wiser than myself, then I might go to the god with a refutation in my hand. I should say to him, 'Here is a man who is wiser than I am; but you said that I was the wisest.' Accordingly I went to one who had the reputation of wisdom, and observed to him – his name I need not mention; he was a politician whom I selected for examination – and the result was as follows: When I began to talk with him, I could not help thinking that he was not really wise, although he was thought wise by many, and wiser still by himself; and I went and tried to explain to him that he thought himself wise, but was not really wise; and the consequence was that he hated me, and his enmity was shared by several who were present and heard me. So I left him, saying to myself, as I went away: Well, although I do not suppose that either of us knows anything really beautiful and good, I am better off than he is – for he knows nothing, and thinks that he knows. I neither know nor think that I know. In this latter particular, then, I seem to have slightly the advantage of him. Then I went to another, who had still higher philosophical pretensions, and my conclusion was exactly the same. I made another enemy of him, and of many others besides him.

After this I went to one man after another, being not unconscious of the enmity which I provoked, and I lamented and feared this: but necessity was laid upon me – the word of God, I thought, ought to be considered first. And I said to myself, Go I

must to all who appear to know, and find out the meaning of the oracle. And I swear to you, Athenians, by the dog I swear! – for I must tell you the truth – the result of my mission was just this: I found that the men most in repute were all but the most foolish; and that some inferior men were really wiser and better. I will tell you the tale of my wanderings and of the 'Herculean' labours, as I may call them, which I endured only to find at last the oracle irrefutable. When I left the politicians, I went to the poets; tragic, dithyrambic, and all sorts. And there, I said to myself, you will be detected; now you will find out that you are more ignorant than they are. Accordingly, I took them some of the most elaborate passages in their own writings, and asked what was the meaning of them – thinking that they would teach me something. Will you believe me? I am almost ashamed to speak of this, but still I must say that there is hardly a person present who would not have talked better about their poetry than they did themselves. That showed me in an instant that not by wisdom do poets write poetry, but by a sort of genius and inspiration; they are like diviners or soothsayers who also say many fine things, but do not understand the meaning of them. And the poets appeared to me to be much in the same case; and I further observed that upon the strength of their poetry they believed themselves to be the wisest of men in other things in which they were not wise. So I departed, conceiving myself to be superior to them for the same reason that I was superior to the politicians.

At last I went to the artisans, for I was conscious that I knew nothing at all, as I may say, and I was sure that they knew many fine things; and in this I was not mistaken, for they did know many things of which I was ignorant, and in this they certainly were wiser than I was. But I observed that even the good artisans fell into the same error as the poets; because they were good workmen they thought that they also knew all sorts of high matters, and this defect in them overshadowed their wisdom – therefore I asked myself on behalf of the oracle, whether I would like to be as I was, neither having their knowledge nor their ignorance, or like them in both;

and I made answer to myself and the oracle that I was better off as I was.

This investigation has led to my having many enemies of the worst and most dangerous kind, and has given occasion also to many calumnies, and I am called wise, for my hearers always imagine that I myself possess the wisdom which I find wanting in others: but the truth is, O men of Athens, that God only is wise; and in this oracle he means to say that the wisdom of men is little or nothing; he is not speaking of Socrates, he is only using my name as an illustration, as if he said, He, O men, is the wisest, who, like Socrates, knows that his wisdom is in truth worth nothing. And so I go my way, obedient to the god, and make inquisition into the wisdom of anyone, whether citizen or stranger, who appears to be wise; and if he is not wise, then in vindication of the oracle I show him that he is not wise; and this occupation quite absorbs me, and I have no time to give either to any public matter of interest or to any concern of my own, but I am in utter poverty by reason of my devotion to the god.

There is another thing: young men of the richer classes, who have not much to do, come about me of their own accord; they like to hear the pretenders examined, and they often imitate me, and examine others themselves; there are plenty of persons, as they soon enough discover, who think that they know something, but

really know little or nothing: and then those who are examined by them instead of being angry with themselves are angry with me: This confounded Socrates, they say; this villainous misleader of youth! – and then if somebody asks them, Why, what

evil does he practise or teach? they do not know, and cannot tell; but in order that they may not appear to be at a loss, they repeat the ready-made charges which are used against all philosophers about teaching things up in the clouds and under the earth, and having no gods, and making the worse appear the better cause; for they do not like to confess that their pretence of knowledge has been detected – which is the truth: and as they are numerous and ambitious and energetic, and are all in battle array and have persuasive tongues, they have filled your ears with their loud and inveterate calumnies. And this is the reason why my three accusers, Meletus and Anytus and Lycon, have set upon me; Meletus, who has a quarrel with me on behalf of the poets; Anytus, on behalf of the craftsmen; Lycon, on behalf of the rhetoricians: and as I said at the beginning, I cannot expect to get rid of this mass of calumny all in a moment. And this, O men of Athens, is the truth and the whole truth; I have concealed nothing, I have dissembled nothing. And yet I know that this plainness of speech makes them hate me, and what is their hatred but a proof that I am speaking the truth? – this is the occasion and reason of their slander of me, as you will find out either in this or in any future inquiry.

I have said enough in my defence against the first class of my accusers; I turn to the second class, who are headed by Meletus, that good and patriotic man, as he calls himself. And now I will try to defend myself against them: these new accusers must also have their affidavit read. What do they say? Something of this sort:– That Socrates is a doer of evil, and corrupter of the youth, and he does not believe in the gods of the state, and has other new divinities of his own. That is the sort of charge; and now let us examine the particular counts. He says that I am a doer of evil, who corrupt the youth; but I say, O men of Athens, that Meletus is a doer of evil, and the evil is that he makes a joke of a serious matter, and is too ready at bringing other men to trial from a pretended zeal and interest about matters in which he really never had the smallest interest. And the truth of this I will endeavour to prove.

Come hither, Meletus, and let me ask a question of you. You think a great deal about the improvement of youth?

Yes, I do.

Tell the judges, then, who is their improver; for you must know, as you have taken the pains to discover their corrupter, and are citing and accusing me before them. Speak, then, and tell the judges who their improver is. Observe, Meletus, that you are silent, and have nothing to say. But is not this rather disgraceful, and a very considerable proof of what I was saying, that you have no interest in the matter? Speak up, friend, and tell us who their improver is.

The laws.

But that, my good sir, is not my meaning. I want to know who the person is, who, in the first place, knows the laws.

The judges, Socrates, who are present in court.

What, do you mean to say, Meletus, that they are able to instruct and improve youth?

Certainly they are.

What, all of them, or some only and not others?

All of them.

By the goddess Here, that is good news! There are plenty of improvers, then. And what do you say of the audience – do they improve them?

Yes, they do.

And the senators?

Yes, the senators improve them.

But perhaps the members of the citizen assembly corrupt them? – or do they too improve them?

They improve them.

Then every Athenian improves and elevates them; all with the exception of myself; and I alone am their corrupter? Is that what you affirm?

That is what I stoutly affirm.

I am very unfortunate if that is true. But suppose I ask you a

APOLOGY

question: Would you say that this also holds true in the case of horses? Does one man do them harm and all the world good? Is not the exact opposite of this true? One man is able to do them good, or at least not many; – the trainer of horses, that is to say, does them good, and others who have to do with them rather injure them? Is not that true, Meletus, of horses, or any other animals? Yes, certainly. Whether you and Anytus say yes or no, that is no matter. Happy indeed would be the condition of youth if they had one corrupter only, and all the rest of the world were their improvers. And you, Meletus, have sufficiently shown that you never had a thought about the young: your carelessness is seen in your not caring about matters spoken of in this very indictment.

And now, Meletus, I must ask you another question: Which is better, to live among bad citizens, or among good ones? Answer, friend, I say; for that is a question which may be easily answered. Do not the good do their neighbours good, and the bad do them evil?

Certainly.

And is there anyone who would rather be injured than benefited by those who live with him? Answer, my good friend; the law requires you to answer – does anyone like to be injured?

Certainly not.

And when you accuse me of corrupting and deteriorating the youth, do you allege that I corrupt them intentionally or unintentionally?

Intentionally, I say.

But you have just admitted that the good do their neighbours good, and the evil do them evil. Now is that a truth which your superior wisdom has recognized thus early in life, and am I, at my age, in such darkness and ignorance as not to know that if a man with whom I have to live is corrupted by me, I am very likely to be harmed by him, and yet I corrupt him, and intentionally, too; – that is what you are saying, and of that you will never persuade me or any other human being. But either I do not corrupt them, or I corrupt them unintentionally, so that on either view of the case you lie. If my offence is unintentional, the law has no cognizance of unintentional offences: you ought to have taken me privately, and warned and admonished me; for if I had been better advised, I should have left off doing what I only did unintentionally – no doubt I should; whereas you hated to converse with me or teach me, but you indicted me in this court, which is a place not of instruction, but of punishment.

I have shown, Athenians, as I was saying, that Meletus has no care at all, great or small, about the matter. But still I should like to know, Meletus, in what I am affirmed to corrupt the young. I suppose you mean, as I infer from your indictment, that I teach them not to acknowledge the gods which the state acknowledges, but some other new divinities or spiritual agencies in their stead. These are the lessons which corrupt the youth, as you say.

Yes, that I say emphatically.

Then, by the gods, Meletus, of whom we are speaking, tell me and the court, in somewhat plainer terms, what you mean! for I do not as yet understand whether you affirm that I teach others to acknowledge some gods, and therefore do believe in gods and am not an entire atheist – this you do not lay to my charge; but only that they are not the same gods which the city recognizes – the charge is that they are different gods. Or, do you mean to say that I am an atheist simply, and a teacher of atheism?

I mean the latter – that you are a complete atheist.

That is an extraordinary statement, Meletus. Why do you say that? Do you mean that I do not believe in the godhead of the sun or moon, which is the common creed of all men?

I assure you, judges, that he does not believe in them; for he says that the sun is stone, and the moon earth.

Friend Meletus, you think that you are accusing Anaxagoras; and you have but a bad opinion of the judges, if you fancy them ignorant to such a degree as not to know that those doctrines are found in the books of Anaxagoras the Clazomenian, who is full of them. And these are the doctrines which the youth are said to learn

of Socrates, when there are not unfrequently exhibitions of them at the theatre (price of admission one drachma at the most); and they might cheaply purchase them, and laugh at Socrates if he pretends to father such eccentricities. And so, Meletus, you really think that I do not believe in any god?

I swear by Zeus that you believe absolutely in none at all.

You are a liar, Meletus, not believed even by yourself. For I cannot help thinking, O men of Athens, that Meletus is reckless and impudent, and that he has written this indictment in a spirit of mere wantonness and youthful bravado. Has he not compounded a riddle, thinking to try me? He said to himself: I shall see whether this wise Socrates will discover my ingenious contradiction, or whether I shall be able to deceive him and the rest of them. For he certainly does appear to me to contradict himself in the indictment as much as if he said that Socrates is guilty of not believing in the gods, and yet of believing in them – but this surely is a piece of fun.

I should like you, O men of Athens, to join me in examining what I conceive to be his inconsistency; and do you, Meletus, answer. And I must remind you that you are not to interrupt me if I speak in my accustomed manner.

Did ever man, Meletus, believe in the existence of human things, and not of human beings?… I wish, men of Athens, that he would answer, and not be always trying to get up an interruption. Did ever any man believe in horsemanship, and not in horses? or in flute-playing, and not in flute-players? No, my friend; I will answer to you and to the court, as you refuse to answer for yourself. There is no man who ever did. But now please to answer the next question: Can a man believe in spiritual and divine agencies, and

not in spirits or demigods?

He cannot.

I am glad that I have extracted that answer, by the assistance of the court; nevertheless you swear in the indictment that I teach and believe in divine or spiritual agencies (new or old, no matter for that); at any rate, I believe in spiritual agencies, as you say and swear in the affidavit; but if I believe in divine beings, I must believe in spirits or demigods; – is not that true? Yes, that is true, for I may assume that your silence gives assent to that. Now what are spirits or demigods? are they not either gods or the sons of gods? Is that true?

Yes, that is true.

But this is just the ingenious riddle of which I was speaking: the demigods or spirits are gods, and you say first that I don't believe in gods, and then again that I do believe in gods; that is, if I believe in demigods. For if the demigods are the illegitimate sons of gods, whether by the Nymphs or by any other mothers, as is thought, that, as all men will allow, necessarily implies the existence of their parents. You might as well affirm the existence of mules, and deny that of horses and asses. Such nonsense, Meletus, could only have been intended by you as a trial of me. You have put this into the indictment because you had nothing real of which to accuse me. But no one who has a particle of understanding will ever be convinced by you that the same man can believe in divine and superhuman things, and yet not believe that there are gods and demigods and heroes.

I have said enough in answer to the charge of Meletus: any elaborate defence is unnecessary; but as I was saying before, I certainly have many enemies, and this is what will be my destruction if I am destroyed; of that I am certain; – not Meletus,

nor yet Anytus, but the envy and detraction of the world, which has been the death of many good men, and will probably be the death of many more; there is no danger of my being the last of them.

Someone will say: And are you not ashamed, Socrates, of a course of life which is likely to bring you to an untimely end? To him I may fairly answer: There you are mistaken: a man who is good for anything ought not to calculate the chance of living or dying; he ought only to consider whether in doing anything he is doing right or wrong – acting the part of a good man or of a bad. Whereas, according to your view, the heroes who fell at Troy were not good for much, and the son of Thetis above all, who altogether despised danger in comparison with disgrace; and when his goddess mother said to him, in his eagerness to slay Hector, that if he avenged his companion Patroclus, and slew Hector, he would die himself – 'Fate,' as she said, 'waits upon you next after Hector'; he, hearing this, utterly despised danger and death, and instead of fearing them, feared rather to live in dishonour, and not to avenge his friend. 'Let me die next,' he replies, 'and be avenged of my enemy, rather than abide here by the beaked ships, a scorn and a burden of the earth.' Had Achilles any thought of death and danger? For wherever a man's place is, whether the place which he has chosen or that in which he has been placed by a commander, there he ought to remain in the hour of danger; he should not think of death or of anything, but of disgrace. And this, O men of Athens, is a true saying.

Strange, indeed, would be my conduct, O men of Athens, if I who, when I was ordered by the generals whom you chose to command me at Potidaea and Amphipolis and Delium, remained where they placed me, like any other man, facing death; if, I say, now, when, as I conceive and imagine, God orders me to fulfil the philosopher's mission of searching into myself and other men, I were to desert my post through fear of death, or any other fear; that would indeed be strange, and I might justly be arraigned in court for denying the existence of the gods, if I disobeyed the oracle because I was afraid of death: then I should be fancying that I was wise when I was not wise. For this fear of death is indeed the pretence of wisdom, and not real wisdom, being the appearance of knowing the unknown; since no one knows whether death, which they in their fear apprehend to be the greatest evil, may not be the greatest good. Is there not here conceit of knowledge, which is a disgraceful sort of ignorance? And this is the point in which, as I think, I am superior to men in general, and in which I might perhaps fancy myself wiser than other men – that whereas I know but little of the world below, I do not suppose that I know: but I do know that injustice and disobedience to a better, whether God or man, is evil and dishonourable, and I will never fear or avoid a possible good rather than a certain evil. And therefore if you let me go now, and reject the counsels of Anytus, who said that if I were not put to death I ought not to have been prosecuted, and that if I escape now, your sons will all be utterly ruined by listening to my words – if you say to me, Socrates, this time we will not mind Anytus, and will let you off, but upon one condition, that you are not to inquire and speculate in this way any more, and that if you are caught doing this again you shall die; – if this was the condition on which you let me go, I should reply: Men of Athens, I honour and love you; but I shall obey God rather than you, and while I have life and strength I shall never cease from the practice and teaching of philosophy, exhorting anyone whom I meet after my manner, and convincing him, saying: O my friend, why do you who are a citizen of the great and mighty and wise city of Athens, care so much about laying up the greatest amount of money and honour and reputation, and so little about wisdom and truth and the greatest improvement of the soul, which you never regard or heed at all? Are you not ashamed of this? And if the person with whom I am arguing says: Yes, but I do care; I do not depart or let him go at once; I interrogate and examine and cross-examine him, and if I think that he has no virtue, but only says that he has, I reproach him with undervaluing the greater, and overvaluing the less. And this I

should say to everyone whom I meet, young and old, citizen and alien, but especially to the citizens, inasmuch as they are my brethren. For this is the command of God, as I would have you know; and I believe that to this day no greater good has ever happened in the state than my service to the God. For I do nothing but go about persuading you all, old and young alike, not to take thought for your persons and your properties, but first and chiefly to care about the greatest improvement of the soul. I tell you that virtue is not given by money, but that from virtue come money and every other good of man, public as well as private. This is my teaching, and if this is the doctrine which corrupts the youth, my influence is ruinous indeed. But if anyone says that this is not my teaching, he is speaking an untruth. Wherefore, O men of Athens, I say to you, do as Anytus bids or not as Anytus bids, and either acquit me or not; but whatever you do, know that I shall never alter my ways, not even if I have to die many times.

Men of Athens, do not interrupt, but hear me; there was an agreement between us that you should hear me out. And I think that what I am going to say will do you good: for I have something more to say, at which you may be inclined to cry out; but I beg that you will not do this. I would have you know that, if you kill such a one as I am, you will injure yourselves more than you will injure me. Meletus and Anytus will not injure me: they cannot; for it is not in the nature of things that a bad man should injure a better than himself. I do not deny that he may, perhaps, kill him, or drive him into exile, or deprive him of civil rights; and he may imagine, and others may imagine, that he is doing him a great injury: but in that I do not agree with him; for the evil of doing as Anytus is doing – of unjustly taking away another man's life – is greater far. And now, Athenians, I am not going to argue for my own sake, as you may think, but for yours, that you may not sin against the God, or lightly reject his boon by condemning me. For if you kill me you will not easily find another like me, who, if I may use such a ludicrous figure of speech, am a sort of gadfly, given to the state by the God; and the state is like a great and noble steed who is tardy in his motions owing to his very size, and requires to be stirred into life. I am that gadfly which God has given the state and all day long and in all places am always fastening upon you, arousing and persuading and reproaching you. And as you will not easily find another like me, I would advise you to spare me. I dare say that you may feel irritated at being suddenly awakened when you are caught napping; and you may think that if you were to strike me dead, as Anytus advises, which you easily might, then you would sleep on for the remainder of your lives, unless God in his care of you gives you another gadfly. And that I am given to you by God is proved by this: that if I had been like other men, I should not have neglected all my own concerns, or patiently seen the neglect of them during all these years, and have been doing yours, coming to you individually, like a father or elder brother, exhorting you to regard virtue; this, I say, would not be like human nature. And had I gained anything, or if my exhortations had been paid, there would have been some sense in that: but now, as you will perceive, not even the impudence of my accusers dares to say that I have ever exacted or sought pay of anyone; they have no witness of that. And I have a witness of the truth of what I say; my poverty is a sufficient witness.

Someone may wonder why I go about in private, giving advice and busying myself with the concerns of others, but do not venture to come forward in public and advise the state. I will tell you the reason of this. You have often heard me speak of an oracle or sign which comes to me, and is the divinity which Meletus ridicules in the indictment. This sign I have had ever since I was a child. The sign is a voice which comes to me and always forbids me to do something which I am going to do, but never commands me to do anything, and this is what stands in the way of my being a politician. And rightly, as I think. For I am certain, O men of Athens, that if I had engaged in politics, I should have perished long ago and done no good either to you or to myself. And don't be offended at my telling you the truth: for the truth is that no man who goes to war with you or any other multitude, honestly struggling against the commission of unrighteousness and wrong in the state, will save his life; he who will really fight for the right, if he would live even for a little while, must have a private station and not a public one.

I can give you as proofs of this, not words only, but deeds, which you value more than words. Let me tell you a passage of my own life, which will prove to you that I should never have yielded to injustice from any fear of death, and that if I had not yielded I should have died at once. I will tell you a story – tasteless, perhaps, and commonplace, but nevertheless true. The only office of state which I ever held, O men of Athens, was that of senator; the tribe Antiochis, which is my tribe, had the presidency at the trial of the generals who had not taken up the bodies of the slain after the battle of Arginusae; and you proposed to try them all together, which was illegal, as you all thought afterwards; but at the time I was the only one of the Prytanes who was opposed to the illegality, and I gave my vote against you; and when the orators threatened to impeach and arrest me, and have me taken away, and you called and shouted, I made up my mind that I would run the risk, having law and justice with me, rather than take part in your injustice because I feared imprisonment and death. This happened in the days of the democracy. But when the oligarchy of the Thirty was in power, they sent for me and four others into the rotunda, and bade us bring Leon the Salaminian from Salamis, as they wanted to execute him. This was a specimen of the sort of commands which they were always giving with the view of implicating as many as possible in their crimes; and then I showed, not in words only, but in deed, that, if I may be allowed to use such an expression, I cared not a straw for death, and that my only fear was the fear of doing an unrighteous or unholy thing. For the strong arm of that oppressive power did not frighten me into doing wrong; and when we came out of the rotunda the other four went to Salamis and fetched Leon, but I went quietly home. For which I might have lost my life, had not the power of the Thirty shortly afterwards come to an end. And to this many will witness.

Now do you really imagine that I could have survived all these years, if I had led a public life, supposing that like a good man I had always supported the right and had made justice, as I ought, the first thing? No, indeed, men of Athens, neither I nor any other. But I have been always the same in all my actions, public as well as private, and never have I yielded any base compliance to those who are slanderously termed my disciples or to any other. For the truth is that I have no regular disciples: but if anyone likes to come and hear me while I am pursuing my mission, whether he be young or old, he may freely come. Nor do I converse with those who pay only, and not with those who do not pay; but anyone, whether he be rich or poor, may ask and answer me and listen to my words; and whether he turns out to be a bad man or a good one, that cannot be justly laid to my charge, as I never taught him anything. And if anyone says that he has ever learned or heard anything from me in private which all the world has not heard, I should like you to know that he is speaking an untruth.

But I shall be asked, Why do people delight in continually conversing with you? I have told you already, Athenians, the whole truth about this: they like to hear the cross-examination of the pretenders to wisdom; there is amusement in this. And this is a duty which the God has imposed upon me, as I am assured by oracles, visions, and in every sort of way in which the will of divine power was ever signified to anyone. This is true, O Athenians; or, if not true, would be soon refuted. For if I am really corrupting the youth, and have corrupted some of them already, those of them who have grown up and have become sensible that I gave them bad advice in the days of their youth should come forward as accusers and take their revenge; and if they do not like to come themselves, some of their relatives, fathers, brothers, or other kinsmen, should say what evil their families suffered at my hands. Now is their time. Many of them I see in the court. There is Crito, who is of the same age and of the same deme with myself; and there is Critobulus his

son, whom I also see. Then again there is Lysanias of Sphettus, who is the father of Aeschines – he is present; and also there is Antiphon of Cephisus, who is the father of Epigenes; and there are the brothers of several who have associated with me. There is Nicostratus the son of Theosdotides, and the brother of Theodotus (now Theodotus himself is dead, and therefore he, at any rate, will not seek to stop him); and there is Paralus the son of Demodocus, who had a brother Theages; and Adeimantus the son of Ariston, whose brother Plato is present; and Aeantodorus, who is the brother of Apollodorus, whom I also see. I might mention a great many others, any of whom Meletus should have produced as witnesses in the course of his speech; and let him still produce them, if he has forgotten – I will make way for him. And let him say, if he has any testimony of the sort which he can produce. Nay, Athenians, the very opposite is the truth. For all these are ready to witness on behalf of the corrupter, of the destroyer of their kindred, as Meletus and Anytus call me; not the corrupted youth only – there might have been a motive for that – but their uncorrupted elder relatives. Why should they too support me with their testimony? Why, indeed, except for the sake of truth and justice, and because they know that I am speaking the truth, and that Meletus is lying.

Well, Athenians, this and the like of this is nearly all the defence which I have to offer. Yet a word more. Perhaps there may be someone who is offended at me, when he calls to mind how he himself, on a similar or even a less serious occasion, had recourse to prayers and supplications with many tears, and how he produced his children in court, which was a moving spectacle, together with a posse of his relations and friends; whereas I, who am probably in danger of my life, will do none of these things. Perhaps this may come into his mind, and he may be set against me, and vote in anger because he is displeased at this. Now if there be such a person among you, which I am far from affirming, I may fairly reply to him: My friend, I am a man, and like other men, a creature of flesh and blood, and not of wood or stone, as Homer says; and I have a family, yes, and sons. O Athenians, three in number, one of whom is growing up, and the two others are still young; and yet I will not bring any of them hither in order to petition you for an acquittal. And why not? Not from any self-will or disregard of you. Whether I am or am not afraid of death is another question, of which I will not now speak. But my reason simply is that I feel such conduct to be discreditable to myself, and you, and the whole state. One who has reached my years, and who has a name for wisdom, whether deserved or not, ought not to debase himself. At any rate, the world has decided that Socrates is in some way superior to other men. And if those among you who are said to be superior in wisdom and courage, and any other virtue, demean themselves in this way, how shameful is their conduct! I have seen men of reputation, when they have been condemned, behaving in the strangest manner: they seemed to fancy that they were going to suffer something dreadful if they died, and that they could be immortal if you only allowed them to live; and I think that they were a dishonour to the state, and that any stranger coming in would say of them that the most eminent men of Athens, to whom the Athenians themselves give honour and command, are no better than women. And I say that these things ought not to be done by those of us who are of reputation; and if they are done, you ought not to permit them; you ought rather to show that you are more inclined to condemn, not the man who is quiet, but the man who gets up a doleful scene, and makes the city ridiculous.

But, setting aside the question of dishonour, there seems to be something wrong in petitioning a judge, and thus procuring an acquittal instead of informing and convincing him. For his duty is, not to make a present of justice, but to give judgement; and he has sworn that he will judge according to the laws, and not according to his own good pleasure; and neither he nor we should get into the habit of perjuring ourselves – there can be no piety in that. Do not then require me to do what I consider dishonourable and impious and wrong, especially now, when I am being tried for impiety on

the indictment of Meletus. For if, O men of Athens, by force of persuasion and entreaty, I could overpower your oaths, then I should be teaching you to believe that there are no gods, and convict myself, in my own defence, of not believing in them. But that is not the case; for I do believe that there are gods, and in a far higher sense than that in which any of my accusers believe in them. And to you and to God I commit my cause, to be determined by you as is best for you and me.

The jury returns a guilty verdict and Socrates responds:

There are many reasons why I am not grieved, O men of Athens, at the vote of condemnation. I expected it, and am only surprised that the votes are so nearly equal; for I had thought that the majority against me would have been far larger; but now, had thirty votes gone over to the other side, I should have been acquitted. And I may say that I have escaped Meletus. And I may say more; for without the assistance of Anytus and Lycon, he would not have had a fifth part of the votes, as the law requires, in which case he would have incurred a fine of a thousand drachmae, as is evident.

And so he proposes death as the penalty. And what shall I propose on my part, O men of Athens? Clearly that which is my due. And what is that which I ought to pay or to receive? What shall be done to the man who has never had the wit to be idle during his whole life; but has been careless of what the many care about – wealth, and family interests, and military offices, and speaking in the assembly, and magistracies, and plots, and parties. Reflecting that I was really too honest a man to follow in this way and live, I did not go where I could do no good to you or to myself; but where I could do the greatest good privately to everyone of you, thither I went, and sought to persuade every man among you that he must look to himself, and seek virtue and wisdom before he looks to his private interests, and look to the state before he looks to the interests of the state; and that this should be the order which he observes in all his actions. What shall be done to such a one? Doubtless some

good thing, O men of Athens, if he has his reward; and the good should be of a kind suitable to him. What would be a reward suitable to a poor man who is your benefactor, who desires leisure that he may instruct you? There can be no more fitting reward than maintenance in the Prytaneum, O men of Athens, a reward which he deserves far more than the citizen who has won the prize at Olympia in the horse or chariot race, whether the chariots were drawn by two horses or by many. For I am in want, and he has enough; and he only gives you the appearance of happiness, and I give you the reality. And if I am to estimate the penalty justly, I say that maintenance in the Prytaneum is the just return.

Perhaps you may think that I am braving you in saying this, as in what I said before about the tears and prayers. But that is not the case. I speak rather because I am convinced that I never intentionally wronged anyone, although I cannot convince you of that – for we have had a short conversation only; but if there were a law at Athens, such as there is in other cities, that a capital cause should not be decided in one day, then I believe that I should have convinced you; but now the time is too short. I cannot in a moment refute great slanders; and, as I am convinced that I never wronged another, I will assuredly not wrong myself. I will not say of myself that I deserve any evil, or propose any penalty. Why should I? Because I am afraid of the penalty of death which Meletus proposes? When I do not know whether death is a good or an evil, why should I propose a penalty which would certainly be an evil? Shall I say imprisonment? And why should I live in prison, and be the slave of the magistrates of the year – of the eleven? Or shall the penalty be a fine, and imprisonment until the fine is paid? There is the same objection. I should have to lie in prison, for money I have none, and I cannot pay. And if I say exile (and this may possibly be the penalty which you will affix), I must indeed be blinded by the love of life if I were to consider that when you, who are my own citizens, cannot endure my discourses and words, and have found them so grievous and odious that you would fain have done with

them, others are likely to endure me. No, indeed, men of Athens, that is not very likely. And what a life should I lead, at my age, wandering from city to city, living in ever-changing exile, and always being driven out! For I am quite sure that into whatever place I go, as here so also there, the young men will come to me; and if I drive them away, their elders will drive me out at their desire: and if I let them come, their fathers and friends will drive me out for their sakes.

Someone will say: Yes, Socrates, but cannot you hold your tongue, and then you may go into a foreign city, and no one will interfere with you? Now I have great difficulty in making you understand my answer to this. For if I tell you that this would be a disobedience to a divine command, and therefore that I cannot hold my tongue, you will not believe that I am serious; and if I say again that the greatest good of man is daily to converse about virtue, and all that concerning which you hear me examining myself and others, and that the life which is unexamined is not worth living – that you are still less likely to believe. And yet what I say is true, although a thing of which it is hard for me to persuade you. Moreover, I am not accustomed to think that I deserve any punishment. Had I money I might have proposed to give you what I had, and have been none the worse. But you see that I have none, and can only ask you to proportion the fine to my means. However, I think that I could afford a mina, and therefore I propose that penalty; Plato, Crito, Critobulus, and Apollodorus, my friends here, bid me say thirty minae, and they will be the sureties. Well then, say thirty minae, let that be the penalty; for that they will be ample security to you.

The jury condemns Socrates to death.
Not much time will be gained, O Athenians, in return for the evil name which you will get from the detractors of the city, who will say that you killed Socrates, a wise man; for they will call me wise even although I am not wise when they want to reproach you. If

you had waited a little while, your desire would have been fulfilled in the course of nature. For I am far advanced in years, as you may perceive, and not far from death. I am speaking now only to those of you who have condemned me to death. And I have another thing to say to them: You think that I was convicted through deficiency of words – I mean, that if I had thought fit to leave nothing undone, nothing unsaid, I might have gained an acquittal. Not so; the deficiency which led to my conviction was not of words – certainly not. But I had not the boldness or impudence or inclination to address you as you would have liked me to address you, weeping and wailing and lamenting, and saying and doing many things which you have been accustomed to hear from others, and which, as I say, are unworthy of me. But I thought that I ought not to do anything common or mean in the hour of danger: nor do I now repent of the manner of my defence, and I would rather die having spoken after my manner, than speak in your manner and live. For neither in war nor yet at law ought any man to use every way of escaping death. For often in battle there is no doubt that if a man will throw away his arms, and fall on his knees before his pursuers, he may escape death; and in other dangers there are other ways of escaping death, if a man is willing to say and do anything. The difficulty, my friends, is not in avoiding death, but in avoiding unrighteousness; for that runs faster than death. I am old and move slowly, and the slower runner has overtaken me, and my accusers are keen and quick, and the faster runner, who is unrighteousness, has overtaken them. And now I depart hence condemned by you to suffer the penalty of death, and they, too, go their ways condemned by the truth to suffer the penalty of villainy and wrong; and I must abide by my award – let them abide by theirs. I suppose that these things may be regarded as fated – and I think that they are well.

And now, O men who have condemned me, I would fain prophesy to you; for I am about to die, and that is the hour in which men are gifted with prophetic power. And I prophesy to you who are my murderers, that immediately after my death punishment far

heavier than you have inflicted on me will surely await you. Me you have killed because you wanted to escape the accuser, and not to give an account of your lives. But that will not be as you suppose: far otherwise. For I say that there will be more accusers of you than there are now; accusers whom hitherto I have restrained: and as they are younger they will be more severe with you, and you will be more offended at them. For if you think that by killing men you can avoid the accuser censuring your lives, you are mistaken; that is not a way of escape which is either possible or honourable; the easiest and noblest way is not to be crushing others, but to be improving yourselves. This is the prophecy which I utter before my departure, to the judges who have condemned me.

Friends, who would have acquitted me, I would like also to talk with you about this thing which has happened, while the magistrates are busy, and before I go to the place at which I must die. Stay then awhile, for we may as well talk with one another while there is time. You are my friends, and I should like to show you the meaning of this event which has happened to me. O my judges – for you I may truly call judges – I should like to tell you of a wonderful circumstance. Hitherto the familiar oracle within me has constantly been in the habit of opposing me even about trifles, if I was going to make a slip or error about anything; and now as you see there has come upon me that which may be thought, and is generally believed to be, the last and worst evil. But the oracle made no sign of opposition, either as I was leaving my house and going out in the morning, or when I was going up into this court, or while I was speaking, at anything which I was going to say; and yet I have often been stopped in the middle of a speech; but now in nothing I either said or did touching this matter has the oracle opposed me. What do I take to be the explanation of this? I will tell you. I regard this as a proof that what has happened to me is a good, and that those of us who think that death is an evil are in error. This is a great proof to me of what I am saying, for the customary sign would surely have opposed me had I been going to evil and not to good.

Let us reflect in another way, and we shall see that there is great reason to hope that death is a good, for one of two things: either death is a state of nothingness and utter unconsciousness, or, as men say, there is a change and migration of the soul from this world to another. Now if you suppose that there is no consciousness, but a sleep like the sleep of him who is undisturbed even by the sight of dreams, death will be an unspeakable gain. For if a person were to select the night in which his sleep was undisturbed even by dreams, and were to compare with this the other days and nights of his life, and then were to tell us how many days and nights he had passed in the course of his life better and more pleasantly than this one, I think that any man, I will not say a private man, but even the great king, will not find many such days or nights, when compared with the others. Now if death is like this, I say that to die is gain; for eternity is then only a single night. But if death is the journey to another place, and there, as men say, all the dead are, what good, O my friends and judges, can be greater than this? If indeed when the pilgrim arrives in the world below, he is delivered from the professors of justice in this world, and finds the true judges who are said to give judgement there, Minos and Rhadamanthus and Aeacus and Triptolemus, and other sons of God who were righteous in their own life, that pilgrimage will be worth making. What would not a man give if he might converse with Orpheus and Musaeus and Hesiod and Homer? Nay, if this be true, let me die again and again. I, too, shall have a wonderful interest in a place where I can converse with Palamedes, and Ajax the son of Telamon, and other heroes of old, who have suffered death through an unjust judgement; and there will be no small pleasure, as I think, in comparing my own sufferings with theirs. Above all, I shall be able to continue my search into true and false knowledge; as in this world, so also in that; I shall find out who is wise, and who pretends to be wise, and is not. What would not a man give, O judges, to be able to examine the leader of the great Trojan expedition; or Odysseus or Sisyphus, or numberless others, men and women too!

What infinite delight would there be in conversing with them and asking them questions! For in that world they do not put a man to death for this; certainly not. For besides being happier in that world than in this, they will be immortal, if what is said is true.

Wherefore, O judges, be of good cheer about death, and know this of a truth – that no evil can happen to a good man, either in life or after death. He and his are not neglected by the gods; nor has my own approaching end happened by mere chance. But I see clearly that to die and be released was better for me; and therefore the oracle gave no sign. For which reason also, I am not angry with my accusers, or my condemners; they have done me no harm, although neither of them meant to do me any good; and for this I may gently blame them.

Still I have a favour to ask of them. When my sons are grown up, I would ask you, O my friends, to punish them; and I would have you trouble them, as I have troubled you, if they seem to care about riches, or anything, more than about virtue; or if they pretend to be something when they are really nothing, – then reprove them, as I have reproved you, for not caring about that for which they ought to care, and thinking that they are something when they are really nothing. And if you do this, I and my sons will have received justice at your hands.

The hour of departure has arrived, and we go our ways – I to die, and you to live. Which is better God only knows.

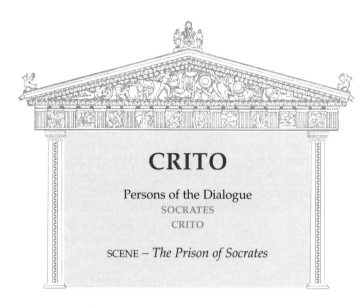

CRITO

Persons of the Dialogue
SOCRATES
CRITO

SCENE – *The Prison of Socrates*

SOCRATES Why have you come at this hour, Crito? it must be quite early?

CRITO Yes, certainly.

SOC. What is the exact time?

CR. The dawn is breaking.

SOC. I wonder the keeper of the prison would let you in.

CR. He knows me because I often come, Socrates; moreover, I have done him a kindness.

SOC. And are you only just come?

CR. No, I came some time ago.

SOC. Then why did you sit and say nothing, instead of awakening me at once?

CR. Why, indeed, Socrates, I myself would rather not have all this sleeplessness and sorrow. But I have been wondering at your peaceful slumbers, and that was the reason why I did not awaken you, because I wanted you to be out of pain. I have always thought you happy in the calmness of your temperament; but never did I see the like of the easy, cheerful way in which you bear this calamity.

SOC. Why, Crito, when a man has reached my age he ought not to

be repining at the prospect of death.

CR. And yet other old men find themselves in similar misfortunes, and age does not prevent them from repining.

SOC. That may be. But you have not told me why you come at this early hour.

CR. I come to bring you a message which is sad and painful; not, as I believe, to yourself but to all of us who are your friends, and saddest of all to me.

SOC. What! I suppose that the ship has come from Delos, on the arrival of which I am to die?

CR. No, the ship has not actually arrived, but she will probably be here to-day, as persons who have come from Sunium tell me that they have left her there; and therefore to-morrow, Socrates, will be the last day of your life.

SOC. Very well, Crito; if such is the will of God, I am willing; but my belief is that there will be a delay of a day.

CR. Why do you say this?

SOC. I will tell you. I am to die on the day after the arrival of the ship?

CR. Yes; that is what the authorities say.

SOC. But I do not think that the ship will be here until to-morrow; this I gather from a vision which I had last night, or rather only just now, when you fortunately allowed me to sleep.

CR. And what was the nature of the vision?

SOC. There came to me the likeness of a woman, fair and comely, clothed in white raiment, who called to me and said: O Socrates, 'The third day hence, to Phthia shalt thou go.'

CR. What a singular dream, Socrates!

SOC. There can be no doubt about the meaning Crito, I think.

CR. Yes: the meaning is only too clear. But, O! my beloved Socrates, let me entreat you once more to take my advice and escape. For if you die I shall not only lose a friend who can never be replaced, but there is another evil: people who do not know you and me will believe that I might have saved you if I had been willing to give

money, but that I did not care. Now, can there be a worse disgrace than this – that I should be thought to value money more than the life of a friend? For the many will not be persuaded that I wanted you to escape, and that you refused.

SOC. But why, my dear Crito, should we care about the opinion of the many? Good men, and they are the only persons who are worth considering, will think of these things truly as they happened.

CR. But do you see, Socrates, that the opinion of the many must be regarded, as is evident in your own case, because they can do the very greatest evil to anyone who has lost their good opinion?

SOC. I only wish, Crito, that they could; for then they could also do the greatest good, and that would be well. But the truth is, that they can do neither good nor evil: they cannot make a man wise or make him foolish; and whatever they do is the result of chance.

CR. Well, I will not dispute about that; but please tell me, Socrates, whether you are not acting out of regard to me and your other friends: are you not afraid that if you escape hence we may get into trouble with the informers for having stolen you away, and lose either the whole or a great part of our property; or that even a worse evil may happen to us? Now, if this is your fear, be at ease; for in order to save you, we ought surely to run this or even a greater risk; be persuaded, then, and do as I say.

SOC. Yes, Crito, that is one fear which you mention, but by no means the only one.

CR. Fear not. There are persons who at no great cost are willing to save you and bring you out of prison; and as for the informers, you may observe that they are far from being exorbitant in their demands; a little money will satisfy them. My means, which, as I am sure, are ample, are at your service, and if you have a scruple

about spending all mine, here are strangers who will give you the use of theirs; and one of them, Simmias the Theban, has brought a sum of money for this very purpose; and Cebes and many others are willing to spend their money too. I say, therefore, do not on that account hesitate about making your escape, and do not say, as you did in the court, that you will have a difficulty in knowing what to do with yourself if you escape. For men will love you in other places to which you may go, and not in Athens only; there are friends of mine in Thessaly, if you like to go to them, who will value and protect you, and no Thessalian will give you any trouble. Nor can I think that you are justified, Socrates, in betraying your own life when you might be saved; this is playing into the hands of your enemies and destroyers; and moreover I should say that you were betraying your children; for you might bring them up and educate them; instead of which you go away and leave them, and they will have to take their chance; and if they do not meet with the usual fate of orphans, there will be small thanks to you. No man should bring children into the world who is unwilling to persevere to the end in their nurture and education. But you are choosing the easier part, as I think, not the better and manlier, which would rather have become one who professes virtue in all his actions, like yourself. And, indeed, I am ashamed not only of you, but of us who are your friends, when I reflect that this entire business of yours will be attributed to our want of courage. The trial need never have come on, or might have been brought to another issue; and the end of all, which is the crowning absurdity, will seem to have been permitted by us, through cowardice and baseness, who might have saved you, as you might have saved yourself, if we had been good for anything (for there was no difficulty in escaping); and we did not see how disgraceful, Socrates, and also miserable all this will be to us as well as to you. Make your mind up then, or rather have your mind already made up, for the time of deliberation is over, and there is only one thing to be done, which must be done, if at all, this very night, and which any delay will render all but impossible; I beseech you therefore, Socrates, to be persuaded by me, and to do as I say.

SOC. Dear Crito, your zeal is invaluable, if a right one; but if wrong, the greater the zeal the greater the evil; and therefore we ought to consider whether these things shall be done or not. For I am and always have been one of those natures who must be guided by reason, whatever the reason may be which upon reflection appears to me to be the best; and now that this fortune has come upon me, I cannot put away the reasons which I have before given: the principles which I have hitherto honoured and revered I still honour, and unless we can find other and better principles on the instant, I am certain not to agree with you; no, not even if the power of the multitude could inflict many more imprisonments, confiscations, deaths, frightening us like children with hobgoblin terrors. But what will be the fairest way of considering the question? Shall I return to your old argument about the opinions of men, some of which are to be regarded, and others, as we were saying, are not to be regarded? Now were we right in maintaining this before I was condemned? And has the argument which was once good now proved to be talk for the sake of talking; in fact an amusement only, and altogether vanity? That is what I want to consider with your help, Crito: whether, under my present circumstances, the argument appears to be in any way different or not; and is to be allowed by me or disallowed. That argument, which, as I believe, is maintained by many who assume to be authorities, was to the effect, as I was saying, that the opinions of some men are to be regarded, and of other men not to be regarded. Now you, Crito, are a disinterested person who are not going to die to-morrow – at least, there is no human probability of this, and you are therefore not liable to be deceived by the circumstances in which you are placed. Tell me, then, whether I am right in saying that some opinions, and the opinions of some men only, are to be valued, and other opinions, and the opinions of other men, are not to be valued. I ask you whether I was right in maintaining this?

CR. Certainly.

SOC. The good are to be regarded, and not the bad?

CR. Yes.

SOC. And the opinions of the wise are good, and the opinions of the unwise are evil?

CR. Certainly.

SOC. And what was said about another matter? Was the disciple in gymnastics supposed to attend to the praise and blame and opinion of every man, or of one man only – his physician or trainer, whoever that was?

CR. Of one man only.

SOC. And he ought to fear the censure and welcome the praise of that one only, and not of the many?

CR. That is clear.

SOC. And he ought to live and train, and eat and drink in the way which seems good to his single master who has understanding, rather than according to the opinion of all other men put together?

CR. True.

SOC. And if he disobeys and disregards the opinion and approval of the one, and regards the opinion of the many who have no understanding, will he not suffer evil?

CR. Certainly he will.

SOC. And what will the evil be, whither tending and what affecting, in the disobedient person?

CR. Clearly, affecting the body; that is what is destroyed by the evil.

SOC. Very good; and is not this true, Crito, of other things which we need not separately enumerate? In the matter of just and unjust, fair and foul, good and evil, which are the subjects of our present consultation, ought we to follow the opinion of the many and to fear them; or the opinion of the one man who has understanding, and whom we ought to fear and reverence more than all the rest of the world: and whom deserting we shall destroy and injure that principle in us which may be assumed to be improved by justice and deteriorated by injustice; is there not such a principle?

CR. Certainly there is, Socrates.

SOC. Take a parallel instance; if, acting under the advice of men who have no understanding, we destroy that which is improvable by health and deteriorated by disease – when that has been destroyed, I say, would life be worth having? And that is – the body?

CR. Yes.

SOC. Could we live, having an evil and corrupted body?

CR. Certainly not.

SOC. And will life be worth having, if that higher part of man be depraved, which is improved by justice and deteriorated by injustice? Do we suppose that principle, whatever it may be in man, which has to do with justice and injustice, to be inferior to the body?

CR. Certainly not.

SOC. More honoured, then?

CR. Far more honoured.

SOC. Then, my friend, we must not regard what the many say of us: but what he, the one man who has understanding of just and unjust, will say, and what the truth will say. And therefore you begin in error when you suggest that we should regard the opinion of the many about just and unjust, good and evil, honourable and dishonourable. Well, someone will say, 'But the many can kill us.'

CR. Yes, Socrates; that will clearly be the answer.

SOC. That is true; but still I find with surprise that the old argument is, as I conceive, unshaken as ever. And I should like to know whether I may say the same of another proposition – that not life, but a good life, is to be chiefly valued?

CR. Yes, that also remains.

SOC. And a good life is equivalent to a just and honourable one – that holds also?

CR. Yes, that holds.

SOC. From these premises I proceed to argue the question whether I ought or ought not to try to escape without the consent of the Athenians: and if I am clearly right in escaping, then I will make the attempt; but if not, I will abstain. The other considerations which you mention, of money and loss of character, and the duty of

educating children, are, I fear, only the doctrines of the multitude, who would be as ready to call people to life, if they were able, as they are to put them to death – and with as little reason. But now, since the argument has thus far prevailed, the only question which remains to be considered is, whether we shall do rightly either in escaping or in suffering others to aid in our escape and paying them in money and thanks, or whether we shall not do rightly; and if the latter, then death or any other calamity which may ensue on my remaining here must not be allowed to enter into the calculation.

CR. I think that you are right, Socrates; how then shall we proceed?

SOC. Let us consider the matter together, and do you either refute me if you can, and I will be convinced; or else cease, my dear friend, from repeating to me that I ought to escape against the wishes of the Athenians: for I am extremely desirous to be persuaded by you, but not against my own better judgement. And now please to consider my first position, and do your best to answer me.

CR. I will do my best.

SOC. Are we to say that we are never intentionally to do wrong, or that in one way we ought and in another way we ought not to do wrong, or is doing wrong always evil and dishonourable, as I was just now saying, and as has been already acknowledged by us? Are all our former admissions which were made within a few days to be thrown away? And have we, at our age, been earnestly discoursing with one another all our life long only to discover that we are no better than children? Or are we to rest assured, in spite of the opinion of the many, and in spite of consequences whether better or worse, of the truth of what was then said, that injustice is always an evil and dishonour to him who acts unjustly? Shall we affirm that?

CR. Yes.

SOC. Then we must do no wrong?

CR. Certainly not.

SOC. Nor when injured injure in return, as the many imagine; for we must injure no one at all?

CR. Clearly not.

SOC. Again, Crito, may we do evil?

CR. Surely not, Socrates.

SOC. And what of doing evil in return for evil, which is the morality of the many – is that just or not?

CR. Not just.

SOC. For doing evil to another is the same as injuring him?

CR. Very true.

SOC. Then we ought not to retaliate or render evil for evil to anyone, whatever evil we may have suffered from him. But I would have you consider, Crito, whether you really mean what you are saying. For this opinion has never been held, and never will be held, by any considerable number of persons; and those who are agreed and those who are not agreed upon this point have no common ground, and can only despise one another, when they see how widely they differ. Tell me, then, whether you agree with and assent to my first principle, that neither injury nor retaliation nor warding off evil by evil is ever right. And shall that be the premise of our agreement? Or do you decline and dissent from this? For this has been of old and is still my opinion; but, if you are of another opinion, let me hear what you have to say. If, however, you remain of the same mind as formerly, I will proceed to the next step.

CR. You may proceed, for I have not changed my mind.

SOC. Then I will proceed to the next step, which may be put in the form of a question: Ought a man to do what he admits to be right, or ought he to betray the right?

CR. He ought to do what he thinks right.

SOC. But if this is true, what is the application? In leaving the prison against the will of the Athenians, do I wrong any? or rather do I not wrong those whom I ought least to wrong? Do I not desert the principles which were acknowledged by us to be just? What do you say?

CR. I cannot tell, Socrates, for I do not know.

SOC. Then consider the matter in this way: Imagine that I am about to play truant (you may call the proceeding by any name which you

like), and the laws and the government come and interrogate me: 'Tell us, Socrates,' they say; 'what are you about? are you going by an act of yours to overturn us – the laws and the whole State, as far as in you lies? Do you imagine that a State can subsist and not be overthrown, in which the decisions of law have no power, but are set aside and overthrown by individuals?' What will be our answer, Crito, to these and the like words? Anyone, and especially a clever rhetorician, will have a good deal to urge about the evil of setting aside the law which requires a sentence to be carried out; and we might reply, 'Yes; but the State has injured us and given an unjust sentence.' Suppose I say that?

CR. Very good, Socrates.

SOC. 'And was that our agreement with you?' the law would say, 'or were you to abide by the sentence of the State?' And if I were to express astonishment at their saying this, the law would probably add: 'Answer, Socrates, instead of opening your eyes: you are in the habit of asking and answering questions. Tell us what complaint you have to make against us which justifies you in attempting to destroy us and the State? In the first place did we not bring you into existence? Your father married your mother by our aid and begat you. Say whether you have any objection to urge against those of us who regulate marriage?' None, I should reply. 'Or against those of us who regulate the system of nurture and education of children in which were trained? Were not the laws, who have the charge of this, right in commanding your father to train you in music and gymnastic?' Right, I should reply. 'Well, then, since you were brought into the world and nurtured and educated by us, can you deny in the first place that you are our child and slave, as your fathers were before you? And if this is true you are not on equal terms with us; nor can you think that you have a right to do to us what we are doing to you. Would you have any right to strike or revile or do any other evil to a father or to your master, if you had one, when you have been struck or reviled by him, or received some other evil at his hands? – you would not say this? And because we think right to destroy you, do you think that you have any right to destroy us in return, and your country as far as in you lies? And will you, O professor of true virtue, say that you are justified in this? Has a philosopher like you failed to discover that our country is more to be valued and higher and holier far than mother or father or any ancestor, and more to be

regarded in the eyes of the gods and of men of understanding? also to be soothed, and gently and reverently entreated when angry, even more than a father, and if not persuaded, obeyed? And when we are punished by her, whether with imprisonment or stripes, the punishment is to be endured in silence; and if she leads us to wounds or death in battle, thither we follow as is right; neither may anyone yield or retreat or leave his rank, but whether in battle or in a court of law, or in any other place, he must do what his city and his country order him; or he must change their view of what is just: and if he may do no violence to his father or mother, much less may he do violence to his country.' What answer shall we make to this, Crito? Do the laws speak truly, or do they not?

CR. I think that they do.

SOC. Then the laws will say: 'Consider, Socrates, if this is true, that in your present attempt you are going to do us wrong. For, after having brought you into the world, and nurtured and educated you, and given you and every other citizen a share in every good that we had to give, we further proclaim and give the right to every Athenian, that if he does not like us when he has come of age and has seen the ways of the city, and made our acquaintance, he may go where he pleases and take his goods with him; and none of us laws will forbid him or interfere with him. Any of you who does not like us and the city, and who wants to go to a colony or to any other city, may go where he likes, and take his goods with him. But he who has experience of the manner in which we order justice and administer the State, and still remains, has entered into an implied contract that he will do as we command him. And he who disobeys us is, as we maintain, thrice wrong: first, because in disobeying us he is disobeying his parents; secondly, because we are the authors of his education; thirdly, because he has made an agreement with us that he will duly obey our commands; and he neither obeys them nor convinces us that our commands are wrong; and we do not rudely impose them, but give him the alternative of obeying or convincing us; that is what we offer and he does neither. These are the sort of accusations to which, as we were saying, you, Socrates, will be exposed if you accomplish your intentions; you, above all other Athenians.' Suppose I ask, why is this? they will justly retort upon me that I above all other men have acknowledged the agreement. 'There is clear proof,' they will say, 'Socrates, that we and the city were not displeasing to you. Of all Athenians you have been the most constant resident in the city, which, as you never leave, you may be supposed to love. For you never went out of the city either to see the games, except once when you went to the Isthmus, or to any other place unless when you were on military service; nor did you travel as other men do. Nor had you any curiosity to know other States or their laws: your affections did not go beyond us and our State; we were your especial favourites, and you acquiesced in our government of you; and this is the State in which you begat your children, which is a proof of your satisfaction. Moreover, you might, if you had liked, have fixed the penalty at banishment in the course of the trial – the State which refuses to let you go now would have let you go then. But you pretended that you preferred death to exile, and that you were not grieved at death. And now you have forgotten these fine sentiments, and pay no respect to us, the laws, of whom you are the destroyer; and are doing what only a miserable slave would do, running away and turning your back upon the compacts and agreements which you made as a citizen. And first of all answer this very question: Are we right in saying that you agreed to be governed according to us in deed, and not in word only? Is that true or not?' How shall we answer that, Crito? Must we not agree?

CR. There is no help, Socrates.

SOC. Then will they not say: 'You, Socrates, are breaking the covenants and agreements which you made with us at your leisure, not in any haste or under any compulsion or deception, but having had seventy years to think of them, during which time you were at liberty to leave the city, if we were not to your mind, or if our covenants appeared to you to be unfair. You had your choice, and might have gone either to Lacedaemon or Crete, which you often praise for their good government, or to some other Hellenic or foreign State. Whereas you, above all other Athenians, seemed to be so fond of the State, or, in other words, of us her laws (for who would like a State that has no laws?), that you never stirred out of her: the halt, the blind, the maimed, were not more stationary in her than you were. And now you run away and forsake your agreements. Not so, Socrates, if you will take our advice; do not make yourself ridiculous by escaping out of the city.

'For just consider, if you transgress and err in this sort of way, what good will you do, either to yourself or to your friends? That your friends will be driven into exile and deprived of citizenship, or will lose their property, is tolerably certain; and you yourself, if you fly to one of the neighbouring cities, as, for example, Thebes or Megara, both of which are well-governed cities, will come to them as an enemy, Socrates, and their government will be against you, and all patriotic citizens will cast an evil eye upon you as a subverter of the laws, and you will confirm in the minds of the judges the justice of their own condemnation of you. For he who is a corrupter of the laws is more than likely to be corrupter of the young and foolish portion of mankind. Will you then flee from well-ordered cities and virtuous men? and is existence worth having on these terms? Or will you go to them without shame, and

talk to them, Socrates? And what will you say to them? What you say here about virtue and justice and institutions and laws being the best things among men? Would that be decent of you? Surely not. But if you go away from well-governed States to Crito's friends in Thessaly, where there is great disorder and license, they will be charmed to have the tale of your escape from prison, set off with ludicrous particulars of the manner in which you were wrapped in a goatskin or some other disguise, and metamorphosed as the fashion of runaways is – that is very likely; but will there be no one to remind you that in your old age you violated the most sacred laws from a miserable desire of a little more life? Perhaps not, if you keep them in a good temper; but if they are out of temper you will hear many degrading things; you will live, but how? – as the flatterer of all men, and the servant of all men; and doing what? – eating and drinking in Thessaly, having gone abroad in order that you may get a dinner. And where will be your fine sentiments about justice and virtue then? Say that you wish to live for the sake of your children, that you may bring them up and educate them –

will you take them into Thessaly and deprive them of Athenian citizenship? Is that the benefit which you would confer upon them? Or are you under the impression that they will be better cared for and educated here if you are still alive, although absent from them; for that your friends will take care of them? Do you fancy that if you are an inhabitant of Thessaly they will take care of them, and if you are an inhabitant of the other world they will not take care of them? Nay; but if they who call themselves friends are truly friends, they surely will.

'Listen, then, Socrates, to us who have brought you up. Think not of life and children first, and of justice afterwards, but of justice first, that you may be justified before the princes of the world below. For neither will you nor any that belong to you be happier or holier or juster in this life, or happier in another, if you do as Crito bids. Now you depart in innocence, a sufferer and not a doer of evil; a victim, not of the laws, but of men. But if you go forth, returning evil for evil, and injury for injury, breaking the covenants and agreements which you have made with us, and wronging those whom you ought least to wrong, that is to say, yourself, your friends, your country, and us, we shall be angry with you while you live, and our brethren, the laws in the world below, will receive you as an enemy; for they will know that you have done your best to destroy us. Listen, then, to us and not to Crito.'

This is the voice which I seem to hear murmuring in my ears, like the sound of the flute in the ears of the mystic; that voice, I say, is humming in my ears, and prevents me from hearing any other. And I know that anything more which you will say will be in vain. Yet speak, if you have anything to say.

CR. I have nothing to say, Socrates.

SOC. Then let me follow the intimations of the will of God.

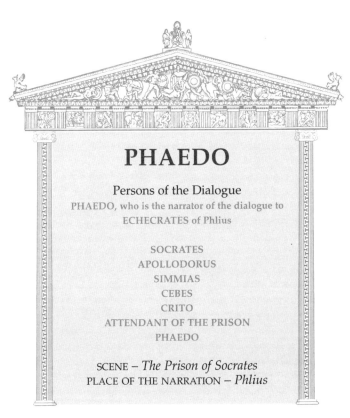

PHAEDO

Persons of the Dialogue

PHAEDO, who is the narrator of the dialogue to
ECHECRATES of Phlius

SOCRATES
APOLLODORUS
SIMMIAS
CEBES
CRITO
ATTENDANT OF THE PRISON
PHAEDO

SCENE – *The Prison of Socrates*
PLACE OF THE NARRATION – *Phlius*

ECHECRATES Were you yourself, Phaedo, in the prison with
Socrates on the day when he drank the poison?

PHAEDO Yes, Echecrates, I was.

ECH. I wish that you would tell me about his death. What did he
say in his last hours? We were informed that he died by taking
poison, but no one knew anything more; for no Phliasian ever goes
to Athens now, and a long time has elapsed since any Athenian
found his way to Phlius, and therefore we had no clear account.

PHAED. Did you not hear of the proceedings at the trial?

ECH. Yes; someone told us about the trial, and we could not
understand why, having been condemned, he was put to death, as

appeared, not at the time, but long afterwards. What was the reason of this?

PHAED. An accident, Echecrates. The reason was that the stern of the ship which the Athenians send to Delos happened to have been crowned on the day before he was tried.

ECH. What is this ship?

PHAED. This is the ship in which, as the Athenians say, Theseus went to Crete when he took with him the fourteen youths, and was the saviour of them and of himself. And they were said to have vowed to Apollo at the time, that if they were saved they would make an annual pilgrimage to Delos. Now this custom still continues, and the whole period of the voyage to and from Delos, beginning when the priest of Apollo crowns the stern of the ship, is a holy season, during which the city is not allowed to be polluted by public executions; and often, when the vessel is detained by adverse winds, there may be a very considerable delay. As I was saying, the ship was crowned on the day before the trial, and this was the reason why Socrates lay in prison and was not put to death until long after he was condemned.

ECH. What was the manner of his death, Phaedo? What was said or done? And which of his friends had he with him? Or were they not allowed by the authorities to be present? And did he die alone?

PHAED. No; there were several of his friends with him.

ECH. If you have nothing to do, I wish that you would tell me what passed, as exactly as you can.

PHAED. I have nothing to do, and will try to gratify your wish. For to me, too, there is no greater pleasure than to have Socrates brought to my recollection, whether I speak myself or hear another speak of him.

ECH. You will have listeners who are of the same mind with you, and I hope that you will be as exact as you can.

PHAED. I remember the strange feeling which came over me at being with him. For I could hardly believe that I was present at the death of a friend, and therefore I did not pity him, Echecrates; his

mien and his language were so noble and fearless in the hour of death that to me he appeared blessed. I thought that in going to the other world he could not be without a divine call, and that he would be happy, if any man ever was, when he arrived there, and therefore I did not pity him as might seem natural at such a time. But neither could I feel the pleasure which I usually felt in philosophical discourse (for philosophy was the theme of which we spoke). I was pleased, and I was also pained, because I knew that he was soon to die, and this strange mixture of feeling was shared by us all; we were laughing and weeping by turns, especially the excitable Apollodorus – you know the sort of man?

ECH. Yes.

PHAED. He was quite overcome; and I myself and all of us were greatly moved.

ECH. Who were present?

PHAED. Of native Athenians there were, besides Apollodorus, Critobulus and his father Crito, Hermogenes, Epigenes, Aeschines, and Antisthenes; likewise Ctesippus of the deme of Paeania, Menexenus, and some others; but Plato, if I am not mistaken, was ill.

ECH. Were there any strangers?

PHAED. Yes, there were; Simmias the Theban, and Cebes, and Phaedondes; Euclid and Terpison, who came from Megara.

ECH. And was Aristippus there, and Cleombrotus?

PHAED. No, they were said to be in Aegina.

ECH. Anyone else?

PHAED. I think that these were about all.

ECH. And what was the discourse of which you spoke?

PHAED. I will begin at the beginning, and endeavour to repeat the entire conversation. You must understand that we had been

previously in the habit of assembling early in the morning at the court in which the trial was held, and which is not far from the prison. There we remained talking with one another until the opening of the prison doors (for they were not opened very early), and then went in and generally passed the day with Socrates. On the last morning the meeting was earlier than usual; this was owing to our having heard on the previous evening that the sacred ship had arrived from Delos, and therefore we agreed to meet very early at the accustomed place. On our going to the prison, the jailer who answered the door, instead of admitting us, came out and bade us wait and he would call us. 'For the eleven,' he said, 'are now with Socrates; they are taking off his chains, and giving orders that he is to die to-day.' He soon returned and said that we might come in. On entering we found Socrates just released from chains, and Xanthippe, whom you know, sitting by him, and holding his child in her arms. When she saw us she uttered a cry and said, as women will: 'O Socrates, this is the last time that either you will converse with your friends, or they with you.'

Socrates turned to Crito and said: 'Crito, let someone take her home.' Some of Crito's people accordingly led her away, crying out and beating herself. And when she was gone, Socrates, sitting up on the couch, began to bend and rub his leg, saying, as he rubbed: 'How singular is the thing called pleasure, and how curiously related to pain, which might be thought to be the opposite of it; for they never come to a man together, and yet he who pursues either of them is generally compelled to take the other. They are two, and yet they grow together out of one head or stem; and I cannot help thinking that if Aesop had noticed them, he would have made a fable about God trying to reconcile their strife, and when he could not, he fastened their heads together; and this is the reason why when one comes the other follows, as I find in my own case pleasure comes following after the pain in my leg, which was caused by the chain.'

Upon this Cebes said: 'I am very glad indeed, Socrates, that you mentioned the name of Aesop. For that reminds me of a question which has been asked by others, and was asked of me only the day before yesterday by Evenus the poet, and as he will be sure to ask again, you may as well tell me what I should say to him, if you would like him to have an answer. He wanted to know why you who never before wrote a line of poetry, now that you are in prison are putting Aesop into verse, and also composing that hymn in honor of Apollo.'

'Tell him, Cebes,' he replied, 'that I had no idea of rivalling him or his poems; which is the truth, for I knew that I could not do that. But I wanted to see whether I could purge away a scruple which I felt about certain dreams. In the course of my life I have often had intimations in dreams "that I should make music." The same dream came to me sometimes in one form, and sometimes in another, but always saying the same or nearly the same words: Make and cultivate music, said the dream. And hitherto I had imagined that this was only intended to exhort and encourage me in the study of philosophy, which has always been the pursuit of my life, and is the noblest and best of music. The dream was bidding me to do what I was already doing, in the same way that the competitor in a race is bidden by the spectators to run when he is already running. But I was not certain of this, as the dream might have meant music in the popular sense of the word, and being under sentence of death, and the festival giving me a respite, I thought that I should be safer if I satisfied the scruple, and, in obedience to the dream, composed a few verses before I departed. And first I made a hymn in honor of the god of the festival, and then considering that a poet, if he is really to be a poet or maker, should not only put words together but make stories, and as I have no invention, I took some fables of Aesop, which I had ready at hand and knew, and turned them into verse. Tell Evenus this, and bid him be of good cheer; that I would have him come after me if he be a wise man, and not tarry; and that to-day I am likely to be going, for the Athenians say that I must.'

Simmias said: 'What a message for such a man! having been a frequent companion of his, I should say that, as far as I know him,

he will never take your advice unless he is obliged.'

'Why,' said Socrates, 'is not Evenus a philosopher?'

'I think that he is,' said Simmias.

'Then he, or any man who has the spirit of philosophy, will be willing to die, though he will not take his own life, for that is held not to be right.'

Here he changed his position, and put his legs off the couch on to the ground, and during the rest of the conversation he remained sitting.

'Why do you say,' inquired Cebes, 'that a man ought not to take his own life, but that the philosopher will be ready to follow the dying?'

Socrates replied: 'And have you, Cebes and Simmias, who are acquainted with Philolaus, never heard him speak of this?'

'I never understood him, Socrates.'

'My words, too, are only an echo; but I am very willing to say what I have heard: and indeed, as I am going to another place, I ought to be thinking and talking of the nature of the pilgrimage which I am about to make. What can I do better in the interval between this and the setting of the sun?'

'Then tell me, Socrates, why is suicide held not to be right? as

I have certainly heard Philolaus affirm when he was staying with us at Thebes: and there are others who say the same, although none of them has ever made me understand him.'

'But do your best,' replied Socrates, 'and the day may come when you will understand. I suppose that you wonder why, as most things which are evil may be accidentally good, this is to be the only exception (for may not death, too, be better than life in some cases?) and why, when a man is better dead, he is not permitted to be his own benefactor, but must wait for the hand of another.'

'By Jupiter! yes, indeed,' said Cebes, laughing, and speaking in his native Doric.

'I admit the appearance of inconsistency,' replied Socrates, 'but there may not be any real inconsistency after all in this. There is a doctrine uttered in secret that man is a prisoner who has no right to open the door of his prison and run away; this is a great mystery which I do not quite understand. Yet I, too, believe that the gods are our guardians, and that we are a possession of theirs. Do you not agree?'

'Yes, I agree to that,' said Cebes.

'And if one of your own possessions, an ox or an ass, for example, took the liberty of putting himself out of the way when you had given no intimation of your wish that he should die, would you not be angry with him, and would you not punish him if you could?'

'Certainly,' replied Cebes.

'Then there may be reason in saying that a man should wait, and not take his own life until God summons him, as he is now summoning me.'

'Yes, Socrates,' said Cebes, 'there is surely reason in that. And yet how can you reconcile this seemingly true belief that God is our guardian and we his possessions, with that willingness to die which we were attributing to the philosopher? That the wisest of men should be willing to leave this service in which they are ruled by the gods who are the best of rulers is not reasonable, for surely no wise man thinks that when set at liberty he can take better care of himself than the gods take of him. A fool may perhaps think this – he may argue that he had better run away from his master, not considering that his duty is to remain to the end, and not to run away from the good, and that there is no sense in his running away. But the wise man will want to be ever with him who is better than himself. Now this, Socrates, is the reverse of what was just now said; for upon this view the wise man should sorrow and the

fool rejoice at passing out of life.'

The earnestness of Cebes seemed to please Socrates. 'Here,' said he, turning to us, 'is a man who is always inquiring, and is not to be convinced all in a moment, nor by every argument.'

'And in this case,' added Simmias, 'his objection does appear to me to have some force. For what can be the meaning of a truly wise man wanting to fly away and lightly leave a master who is better than himself? And I rather imagine that Cebes is referring to you; he thinks that you are too ready to leave us, and too ready to leave the gods who, as you acknowledge, are our good rulers.'

'Yes,' replied Socrates; 'there is reason in that. And this indictment you think that I ought to answer as if I were in court?'

'That is what we should like,' said Simmias.

'Then I must try to make a better impression upon you than I did when defending myself before the judges. For I am quite ready to acknowledge, Simmias and Cebes, that I ought to be grieved at death, if I were not persuaded that I am going to other gods who are wise and good (of this I am as certain as I can be of anything of the sort) and to men departed (though I am not so certain of this), who are better than those whom I leave behind; and therefore I do not grieve as I might have done, for I have good hope that there is yet something remaining for the dead, and, as has been said of old, some far better thing for the good than for the evil.'

'But do you mean to take away your thoughts with you, Socrates?' said Simmias. 'Will you not communicate them to us? – the benefit is one in which we too may hope to share. Moreover, if you succeed in convincing us, that will be an answer to the charge against yourself.'

'I will do my best,' replied Socrates. 'But you must first let me hear what Crito wants; he was going to say something to me.'

'Only this, Socrates,' replied Crito. 'The attendant who is to give you the poison has been telling me that you are not to talk much, and he wants me to let you know this; for that by talking heat is increased, and this interferes with the action of the poison;

those who excite themselves are sometimes obliged to drink the poison two or three times.'

'Then,' said Socrates, 'let him mind his business and be prepared to give the poison two or three times, if necessary; that is all.'

'I was almost certain that you would say that,' replied Crito, 'but I was obliged to satisfy him.'

'Never mind him,' he said.

'And now I will make answer to you, O my judges, and show that he who has lived as a true philosopher has reason to be of good cheer when he is about to die, and that after death he may hope to receive the greatest good in the other world. And how this may be, Simmias and Cebes, I will endeavour to explain. For I deem that the true disciple of philosophy is likely to be misunderstood by other men; they do not perceive that he is ever pursuing death and dying; and if this is true, why, having had the desire of death all his life long, should he repine at the arrival of that which he has been always pursuing and desiring?'

Simmias laughed and said, 'Though not in a laughing humour, I swear that I cannot help laughing when I think what the wicked world will say when they hear this. They will say that this is very true, and our people at home will agree with them in saying that the life which philosophers desire is truly death, and that they have found them out to be deserving of the death which they desire.'

'And they are right, Simmias, in saying this, with the exception of the words "They have found them out"; for they have not found out what is the nature of this death which the true philosopher desires, or how he deserves or desires death. But let us leave them and have a word with ourselves: Do we believe that there is such a thing as death?'

'To be sure,' replied Simmias.

'And is this anything but the separation of soul and body? And being dead is the attainment of this separation; when the soul exists in herself, and is parted from the body and the body is parted from the soul – that is death?'

'Exactly: that and nothing else,' he replied.

'And what do you say of another question, my friend, about which I should like to have your opinion, and the answer to which will probably throw light on our present inquiry: Do you think that the philosopher ought to care about the pleasures – if they are to be called pleasures – of eating and drinking?'

'Certainly not,' answered Simmias.

'And what do you say of the pleasures of love – should he care about them?'

'By no means.'

'And will he think much of the other ways of indulging the body – for example, the acquisition of costly raiment, or sandals, or other adornments of the body? Instead of caring about them, does he not rather despise anything more than nature needs? What do you say?'

'I should say the true philosopher would despise them.'

'Would you not say that he is entirely concerned with the soul and not with the body? He would like, as far as he can, to be quit of the body and turn to the soul.'

'That is true.'

'In matters of this sort philosophers, above all other men, may be observed in every sort of way to dissever the soul from the body.'

'That is true.'

'Whereas, Simmias, the rest of the world are of opinion that a life which has no bodily pleasures and no part in them is not worth having; but that he who thinks nothing of bodily pleasures is almost as though he were dead.'

'That is quite true.'

'What again shall we say of the actual acquirement of knowledge? – is the body, if invited to share in the inquiry, a hinderer or a helper? I mean to say, have sight and hearing any truth in them? Are they not, as the poets are always telling us, inaccurate witnesses? and yet, if even they are inaccurate and indistinct, what is to be said of the other senses? – for you will allow

that they are the best of them?'

'Certainly,' he replied.

'Then when does the soul attain truth? – for in attempting to consider anything in company with the body she is obviously deceived.'

'Yes, that is true.'

'Then must not existence be revealed to her in thought, if at all?'

'Yes.'

'And thought is best when the mind is gathered into herself and none of these things trouble her – neither sounds nor sights nor pain nor any pleasure – when she has as little as possible to do with the body, and has no bodily sense or feeling, but is aspiring after being?'

'That is true.'

'And in this the philosopher dishonours the body; his soul runs away from the body and desires to be alone and by herself?'

'That is true.'

'Well, but there is another thing, Simmias: Is there or is there not an absolute justice?'

'Assuredly there is.'

'And an absolute beauty and absolute good?'

'Of course.'

'But did you ever behold any of them with your eyes?'

'Certainly not.'

'Or did you ever reach them with any other bodily sense? (and I speak not of these alone, but of absolute greatness, and health, and strength, and of the essence or true nature of everything). Has the reality of them ever been perceived by you through the bodily organs? or rather, is not the nearest approach to the knowledge of their several natures made by him who so orders his intellectual vision as to have the most exact conception of the essence of that which he considers?'

'Certainly.'

'And he attains to the knowledge of them in their highest purity who goes to each of them with the mind alone, not allowing when in the act of thought the intrusion or introduction of sight or any other sense in the company of reason, but with the very light of the mind in her clearness penetrates into the very fight of truth in each; he has got rid, as far as he can, of eyes and ears and of the whole body, which he conceives of only as a disturbing element, hindering the soul from the acquisition of knowledge when in company with her – is not this the sort of man who, if ever man did, is likely to attain the knowledge of existence?'

'There is admirable truth in that, Socrates,' replied Simmias.

'And when they consider all this, must not true philosophers make a reflection, of which they will speak to one another in such words as these: We have found, they will say, a path of speculation which seems to bring us and the argument to the conclusion that while we are in the body, and while the soul is mingled with this mass of evil, our desire will not be satisfied, and our desire is of the truth. For the body is a source of endless trouble to us by reason of the mere requirement of food; and also is liable to diseases which overtake and impede us in the search after truth: and by filling us so full of loves, and lusts, and fears, and fancies, and idols, and every sort of folly, prevents our ever having, as people say, so much as a thought. For whence come wars, and fightings, and factions? whence but from the body and the lusts of the body? For wars are occasioned by the love of money, and money has to be acquired for the sake and in the service of the body; and in consequence of all these things the time which ought to be given to philosophy is lost. Moreover, if there is time and an inclination toward philosophy, yet the body introduces a turmoil and confusion and fear into the course of speculation, and hinders us from seeing the truth: and all experience shows that if we would have pure knowledge of anything we must be quit of the body, and the soul in herself must behold all things in themselves: then I suppose that we shall attain that which we desire, and of which we say that we are lovers, and that is wisdom, not while we live, but after death, as the argument shows; for if while in company with the body the soul cannot have pure knowledge, one of two things seems to follow – either knowledge is not to be attained at all, or, if at all, after death. For then, and not till then, the soul will be in herself alone and without the body. In this present life, I reckon that we make the nearest approach to knowledge when we have the least possible concern or interest in the body, and are not saturated with the bodily nature, but remain pure until the hour when God himself is pleased to release us. And then the foolishness of the body will be cleared away and we shall be pure and hold converse with other pure souls, and know of ourselves the clear light everywhere; and this is surely the light of truth. For no impure thing is allowed to approach the pure. These are the sort of words, Simmias, which the true lovers of wisdom cannot help saying to one another, and thinking. You will agree with me in that?'

'Certainly, Socrates.'

'But if this is true, O my friend, then there is great hope that, going whither I go, I shall there be satisfied with that which has been the chief concern of you and me in our past lives. And now that the hour of departure is appointed to me, this is the hope with which I depart, and not I only, but every man who believes that he has his mind purified.

'Certainly,' replied Simmias.

'And what is purification but the separation of the soul from the body, as I was saying before; the habit of the soul gathering and collecting herself into herself, out of all the courses of the body; the dwelling in her own place alone, as in another life, so also in this, as far as she can; the release of the soul from the chains of the body?'

'Very true,' he said.

'And what is that which is termed death, but this very separation and release of the soul from the body?'

'To be sure,' he said.

'And the true philosophers, and they only, study and are eager to release the soul. Is not the separation and release of the soul from the body their especial study?'

'That is true.'

'And as I was saying at first, there would be a ridiculous contradiction in men studying to live as nearly as they can in a state of death, and yet repining when death comes.'

'Certainly.'

'Then, Simmias, as the true philosophers are ever studying death, to them, of all men, death is the least terrible. Look at the matter in this way: how inconsistent of them to have been always enemies of the body, and wanting to have the soul alone, and when this is granted to them, to be trembling and repining; instead of rejoicing at their departing to that place where, when they arrive, they hope to gain that which in life they loved (and this was wisdom), and at the same time to be rid of the company of their enemy. Many a man has been willing to go to the world below in the hope of seeing there an earthly love, or wife, or son, and conversing with them. And will he who is a true lover of wisdom, and is persuaded in like manner that only in the world below he can worthily enjoy her, still repine at death? Will he not depart with joy? Surely he will, my friend, if he be a true philosopher. For he will have a firm conviction that there only, and nowhere else, he can find wisdom in her purity. And if this be true, he would be very absurd, as I was saying, if he were to fear death.'

'He would indeed,' replied Simmias.

'And when you see a man who is repining at the approach of death, is not his reluctance a sufficient proof that he is not a lover of wisdom, but a lover of the body, and probably at the same time a lover of either money or power, or both?'

'That is very true,' he replied.

'There is a virtue, Simmias, which is named courage. Is not that a special attribute of the philosopher?'

'Certainly.'

'Again, there is temperance. Is not the calm, and control, and disdain of the passions which even the many call temperance, a quality belonging only to those who despise the body and live in

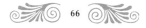

philosophy?'

'That is not to be denied.'

'For the courage and temperance of other men, if you will consider them, are really a contradiction.'

'How is that, Socrates?'

'Well,' he said, 'you are aware that death is regarded by men in general as a great evil.'

'That is true,' he said.

'And do not courageous men endure death because they are afraid of yet greater evils?'

'That is true.'

'Then all but the philosophers are courageous only from fear, and because they are afraid; and yet that a man should be courageous from fear, and because he is a coward, is surely a strange thing.'

'Very true.'

'And are not the temperate exactly in the same case? They are temperate because they are intemperate – which may seem to be a contradiction, but is nevertheless the sort of thing which happens with this foolish temperance. For there are pleasures which they must have, and are afraid of losing; and therefore they abstain from one class of pleasures because they are overcome by another: and whereas intemperance is defined as "being under the dominion of pleasure," they overcome only because they are overcome by pleasure. And that is what I mean by saying that they are temperate through intemperance.'

'That appears to be true.'

'Yet the exchange of one fear or pleasure or pain for another fear or pleasure or pain, which are measured like coins, the greater with the less, is not the exchange of virtue. O my dear Simmias, is there not one true coin for which all things ought to exchange? – and that is wisdom; and only in exchange for this, and in company with this, is anything truly bought or sold, whether courage or temperance or justice. And is not all true virtue the companion of

wisdom, no matter what fears or pleasures or other similar goods or evils may or may not attend her? But the virtue which is made up of these goods, when they are severed from wisdom and exchanged with one another, is a shadow of virtue only, nor is there any freedom or health or truth in her; but in the true exchange there is a purging away of all these things, and temperance, and justice, and courage, and wisdom herself are a purgation of them. And I conceive that the founders of the mysteries had a real meaning and were not mere triflers when they intimated in a figure long ago that he who passes unsanctified and uninitiated into the world below will live in a slough, but that he who arrives there after initiation and purification will dwell with the gods. For "many," as they say in the mysteries, "are the thyrsus-bearers, but few are the mystics," – meaning, as I interpret the words, the true philosophers. In the number of whom I have been seeking, according to my ability, to find a place during my whole life; whether I have sought in a right way or not, and whether I have succeeded or not, I shall truly know in a little while, if God will, when I myself arrive in the other world: that is my belief. And now, Simmias and Cebes, I have answered those who charge me with not grieving or repining at parting from you and my masters in this world; and I am right in not repining, for I believe that I shall find other masters and friends who are as good in the world below. But all men cannot believe this, and I shall be glad if my words have any more success with you than with the judges of the Athenians.'

Cebes answered: 'I agree, Socrates, in the greater part of what you say. But in what relates to the soul, men are apt to be incredulous; they fear that when she leaves the body her place may be nowhere, and that on the very day of death she may be destroyed and perish – immediately on her release from the body, issuing forth like smoke or air and vanishing away into nothingness. For if she could only hold together and be herself after she was released from the evils of the body, there would be good reason to hope, Socrates, that what you say is true. But much

persuasion and many arguments are required in order to prove that when the man is dead the soul yet exists, and has any force of intelligence.'

'True, Cebes,' said Socrates; 'and shall I suggest that we talk a little of the probabilities of these things?'

'I am sure,' said Cebes, 'that I should greatly like to know your opinion about them.'

'I reckon,' said Socrates, 'that no one who heard me now, not even if he were one of my old enemies, the comic poets, could accuse me of idle talking about matters in which I have no concern. Let us, then, if you please, proceed with the inquiry.'

'Whether the souls of men after death are or are not in the world below, is a question which may be argued in this manner: The ancient doctrine of which I have been speaking affirms that they go from this into the other world, and return hither, and are born from the dead. Now if this be true, and the living come from the dead, then our souls must be in the other world, for if not, how could they be born again? And this would be conclusive, if there were any real evidence that the living are only born from the dead; but if there is no evidence of this, then other arguments will have to be adduced.'

'That is very true,' replied Cebes.

'Then let us consider this question, not in relation to man only, but in relation to animals generally, and to plants, and to everything of which there is generation, and the proof will be easier. Are not all things which have opposites generated out of their opposites? I mean such things as good and evil, just and unjust – and there are innumerable other opposites which are generated out of opposites. And I want to show that this holds universally of all opposites; I mean to say, for example, that anything which becomes greater must become greater after being less.'

'True.'

'And that which becomes less must have been once greater and then become less.'

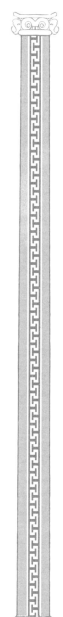

'Yes.'

'And the weaker is generated from the stronger, and the swifter from the slower.'

'Very true.'

'And the worse is from the better, and the more just is from the more unjust.'

'Of course.'

'And is this true of all opposites? and are we convinced that all of them are generated out of opposites?'

'Yes.'

'And in this universal opposition of all things, are there not also two intermediate processes which are ever going on, from one to the other, and back again; where there is a greater and a less there is also an intermediate process of increase and diminution, and that which grows is said to wax, and that which decays to wane?'

'Yes,' he said.

'And there are many other processes, such as division and composition, cooling and heating, which equally involve a passage into and out of one another. And this holds of all opposites, even though not always expressed in words – they are generated out of one another, and there is a passing or process from one to the other of them?'

'Very true,' he replied.

'Well, and is there not an opposite of life, as sleep is the opposite of waking?'

'True,' he said.

'And what is that?'

'Death,' he answered.

'And these, then, are generated, if they are opposites, the one from the other, and have there their two intermediate processes also?'

'Of course.'

'Now,' said Socrates, 'I will analyse one of the two pairs of opposites which I have mentioned to you, and also its intermediate processes, and you shall analyse the other to me. The state of sleep

is opposed to the state of waking, and out of sleeping waking is generated, and out of waking, sleeping, and the process of generation is in the one case falling asleep, and in the other waking up. Are you agreed about that?'

'Quite agreed.'

'Then suppose that you analyse life and death to me in the same manner. Is not death opposed to life?'

'Yes.'

'And they are generated one from the other?'

'Yes.'

'What is generated from life?'

'Death.'

'And what from death?'

'I can only say in answer – life.'

'Then the living, whether things or persons, Cebes, are generated from the dead?'

'That is clear,' he replied.

'Then the inference is, that our souls are in the world below?'

'That is true.'

'And one of the two processes or generations is visible – for surely the act of dying is visible?'

'Surely,' he said.

'And may not the other be inferred as the complement of nature, who is not to be supposed to go on one leg only? And if not, a corresponding process of generation in death must also be assigned to her?'

'Certainly,' he replied.

'And what is that process?'

'Revival.'

'And revival, if there be such a thing, is the birth of the dead into the world of the living?'

'Quite true.'

'Then there is a new way in which we arrive at the inference that the living come from the dead, just as the dead come from the

living; and if this is true, then the souls of the dead must be in some place out of which they come again. And this, as I think, has been satisfactorily proved.'

'Yes, Socrates,' he said; 'all this seems to flow necessarily out of our previous admissions.'

'And that these admissions are not unfair, Cebes,' he said, 'may be shown, as I think, in this way: If generation were in a straight line only, and there were no compensation or circle in nature, no turn or return into one another, then you know that all things would at last have the same form and pass into the same state, and there would be no more generation of them.'

'What do you mean?' he said.

'A simple thing enough, which I will illustrate by the case of sleep,' he replied. 'You know that if there were no compensation of sleeping and waking, the story of the sleeping Endymion would in the end have no meaning, because all other things would be asleep, too, and he would not be thought of. Or if there were composition only, and no division of substances, then the chaos of Anaxagoras would come again. And in like manner, my dear Cebes, if all things which partook of life were to die, and after they were dead remained in the form of death, and did not come to life again, all would at last die, and nothing would be alive – how could this be otherwise? For if the living spring from any others who are not the dead, and they die, must not all things at last be swallowed up in death?'

'There is no escape from that, Socrates,' said Cebes; 'and I think that what you say is entirely true.'

'Yes,' he said, 'Cebes, I entirely think so, too; and we are not walking in a vain imagination; but I am confident in the belief that there truly is such a thing as living again, and that the living spring from the dead, and that the souls of the dead are in existence, and that the good souls have a better portion than the evil.'

Cebes added: 'Your favourite doctrine, Socrates, that knowledge is simply recollection, if true, also necessarily implies a previous time in which we learned that which we now recollect. But

this would be impossible unless our soul was in some place before existing in the human form; here, then, is another argument of the soul's immortality.'

'But tell me, Cebes,' said Simmias, interposing, 'what proofs are given of this doctrine of recollection? I am not very sure at this moment that I remember them.'

'One excellent proof,' said Cebes, 'is afforded by questions. If you put a question to a person in a right way, he will give a true answer of himself; but how could he do this unless there were knowledge and right reason already in him? And this is most clearly shown when he is taken to a diagram or to anything of that sort.'

'But if,' said Socrates, 'you are still incredulous, Simmias, I would ask you whether you may not agree with me when you look at the matter in another way; I mean, if you are still incredulous as to whether knowledge is recollection.'

'Incredulous, I am not,' said Simmias; 'but I want to have this doctrine of recollection brought to my own recollection, and, from what Cebes has said, I am beginning to recollect and be convinced; but I should still like to hear what more you have to say.'

'This is what I would say,' he replied. 'We should agree, if I am not mistaken, that what a man recollects he must have known at some previous time.'

'Very true.'

'And what is the nature of this recollection? And, in asking this, I mean to ask whether, when a person has already seen or heard or in any way perceived anything, and he knows not only that, but something else of which he has not the same, but another knowledge, we may not fairly say that he recollects that which comes into his mind. Are we agreed about that?'

'What do you mean?'

'I mean what I may illustrate by the following instance: The knowledge of a lyre is not the same as the knowledge of a man?'

'True.'

'And yet what is the feeling of lovers when they recognize a

lyre, or a garment, or anything else which the beloved has been in the habit of using? Do not they, from knowing the lyre, form in the mind's eye an image of the youth to whom the lyre belongs? And this is recollection: and in the same way anyone who sees Simmias may remember Cebes; and there are endless other things of the same nature.'

'Yes, indeed, there are – endless,' replied Simmias.

'And this sort of thing,' he said, 'is recollection, and is most commonly a process of recovering that which has been forgotten through time and inattention.'

'Very true,' he said.

'Well; and may you not also from seeing the picture of a horse or a lyre remember a man? and from the picture of Simmias, you may be led to remember Cebes?'

'True.'

'Or you may also be led to the recollection of Simmias himself?'

'True,' he said.

'And in all these cases, the recollection may be derived from things either like or unlike?'

'That is true.'

'And when the recollection is derived from like things, then there is sure to be another question, which is, whether the likeness of that which is recollected is in any way defective or not.'

'Very true,' he said.

'And shall we proceed a step further, and affirm that there is such a thing as equality, not of wood with wood, or of stone with stone, but that, over and above this, there is equality in the abstract? Shall we affirm this?'

'Affirm, yes, and swear to it,' replied Simmias, 'with all the confidence in life.'

'And do we know the nature of this abstract essence?'

'To be sure,' he said.

'And whence did we obtain this knowledge? Did we not see equalities of material things, such as pieces of wood and stones, and

gather from them the idea of an equality which is different from them? – you will admit that? Or look at the matter again in this way: Do not the same pieces of wood or stone appear at one time equal, and at another time unequal?'

'That is certain.'

'But are real equals ever unequal? or is the idea of equality ever inequality?'

'That surely was never yet known, Socrates.'

'Then these (so-called) equals are not the same with the idea of equality?'

'I should say, clearly not, Socrates.'

'And yet from these equals, although differing from the idea of equality, you conceived and attained that idea?'

'Very true,' he said.

'Which might be like, or might be unlike them?'

'Yes.'

'But that makes no difference; whenever from seeing one thing you conceived another, whether like or unlike, there must surely have been an act of recollection?'

'Very true.'

'But what would you say of equal portions of wood and stone, or other material equals? and what is the impression produced by them? Are they equals in the same sense as absolute equality? or do they fall short of this in a measure?'

'Yes,' he said, 'in a very great measure, too.'

'And must we not allow that when I or anyone look at any object, and perceive that the object aims at being some other thing, but falls short of, and cannot attain to it – he who makes this observation must have had previous knowledge of that to which, as he says, the other, although similar, was inferior?'

'Certainly.'

'And has not this been our case in the matter of equals and of absolute equality?'

'Precisely.'

'Then we must have known absolute equality previously to the time when we first saw the material equals, and reflected that all these apparent equals aim at this absolute equality, but fall short of it?'

'That is true.'

'And we recognize also that this absolute equality has only been known, and can only be known, through the medium of sight or touch, or of some other sense. And this I would affirm of all such conceptions.'

'Yes, Socrates, as far as the argument is concerned, one of them is the same as the other.'

'And from the senses, then, is derived the knowledge that all sensible things aim at an idea of equality of which they fall short – is not that true?'

'Yes.'

'Then before we began to see or hear or perceive in any way, we must have had a knowledge of absolute equality, or we could not have referred to that the equals which are derived from the senses – for to that they all aspire, and of that they fall short?'

'That, Socrates, is certainly to be inferred from the previous statements.'

'And did we not see and hear and acquire our other senses as soon as we were born?'

'Certainly.'

'Then must have acquired the knowledge of the ideal equal at some time previous to this?'

'Yes.'

'That is to say, before we were born, I suppose?'

'True.'

'And if we acquired this knowledge before we were born, and were born having it, then we also knew before we were born and at the instant of birth not only equal or the greater or the less, but all other ideas; for we are not speaking only of equality absolute, but of beauty, goodness, justice, holiness, and all which we stamp with

the name of essence in the dialectical process, when we ask and answer questions. Of all this we may certainly affirm that we acquired the knowledge before birth?'

'That is true.'

'But if, after having acquired, we have not forgotten that which we acquired, then we must always have been born with knowledge, and shall always continue to know as long as life lasts – for knowing is the acquiring and retaining knowledge and not forgetting. Is not forgetting, Simmias, just the losing of knowledge?'

'Quite true, Socrates.'

'But if the knowledge which we acquired before birth was lost by us at birth, and afterwards by the use of the senses we recovered that which we previously knew, will not that which we call learning be a process of recovering our knowledge, and may not this be rightly termed recollection by us?'

'Very true.'

'For this is clear, that when we perceived something, either by the help of sight or hearing, or some other sense, there was no difficulty in receiving from this a conception of some other thing like or unlike which had been forgotten and which was associated with this; and therefore, as I was saying, one of two alternatives follows: either we had this knowledge at birth, and continued to know through life; or, after birth, those who are said to learn only remember, and learning is recollection only.'

'Yes, that is quite true, Socrates.'

'And which alternative, Simmias, do you prefer? Had we the knowledge at our birth, or did we remember afterwards the things which we knew previously to our birth?'

'I cannot decide at the moment.'

'At any rate you can decide whether he who has knowledge ought or ought not to be able to give a reason for what he knows.'

'Certainly, he ought.'

'But do you think that every man is able to give a reason about these very matters of which we are speaking?'

'I wish that they could, Socrates, but I greatly fear that to-morrow at this time there will be no one able to give a reason worth having.'

'Then you are not of opinion, Simmias, that all men know these things?'

'Certainly not.'

'Then they are in process of recollecting that which they learned before.'

'Certainly.'

'But when did our souls acquire this knowledge? – not since we were born as men?'

'Certainly not.'

'And therefore previously?'

'Yes.'

'Then, Simmias, our souls must have existed before they were in the form of man – without bodies, and must have had intelligence.'

'Unless indeed you suppose, Socrates, that these notions were given us at the moment of birth; for this is the only time that remains.'

'Yes, my friend, but when did we lose them? for they are not in us when we are born – that is admitted. Did we lose them at the moment of receiving them, or at some other time?'

'No, Socrates, I perceive that I was unconsciously talking nonsense.'

'Then may we not say, Simmias, that if, as we are always repeating, there is an absolute beauty, and goodness, and essence in general, and to this, which is now discovered to be a previous condition of our being, we refer all our sensations, and with this compare them – assuming this to have a prior existence, then our souls must have had a prior existence, but if not, there would be no force in the argument? There can be no doubt that if these absolute ideas existed before we were born, then our souls must have existed before we were born, and if not the ideas, then not the souls.'

'Yes, Socrates; I am convinced that there is precisely the same necessity for the existence of the soul before birth, and of the essence of which you are speaking: and the argument arrives at a result which happily agrees with my own notion. For there is nothing which to my mind is so evident as that beauty, goodness, and other notions of which you were just now speaking have a most real and absolute existence; and I am satisfied with the proof.'

'Well, but is Cebes equally satisfied? for I must convince him too.'

'I think,' said Simmias, 'that Cebes is satisfied: although he is the most incredulous of mortals, yet I believe that he is convinced of the existence of the soul before birth. But that after death the soul will continue to exist is not yet proven even to my own satisfaction. I cannot get rid of the feeling of the many to which Cebes was referring – the feeling that when the man dies the soul may be scattered, and that this may be the end of her. For admitting that she may be generated and created in some other place, and may have existed before entering the human body, why after having entered in and gone out again may she not herself be destroyed and come to an end?'

'Very true, Simmias,' said Cebes; 'that our soul existed before we were born was the first half of the argument, and this appears to have been proven; that the soul will exist after death as well as before birth is the other half of which the proof is still wanting, and has to be supplied.'

'But that proof, Simmias and Cebes, has been already given,' said Socrates, 'if you put the two arguments together – I mean this and the former one, in which we admitted that everything living is born of the dead. For if the soul existed before birth, and in coming to life and being born can be born only from death and dying, must she not after death continue to exist, since she has to be born again? surely the proof which you desire has been already furnished. Still I suspect that you and Simmias would be glad to probe the argument further; like children, you are haunted with a fear that

when the soul leaves the body, the wind may really blow her away and scatter her; especially if a man should happen to die in stormy weather and not when the sky is calm.'

Cebes answered with a smile: 'Then, Socrates, you must argue us out of our fears – and yet, strictly speaking, they are not our fears, but there is a child within us to whom death is a sort of hobgoblin; him too we must persuade not to be afraid when he is alone with him in the dark.'

Socrates said: 'Let the voice of the charmer be applied daily until you have charmed him away.'

'And where shall we find a good charmer of our fears, Socrates, when you are gone?'

'Hellas,' he replied, 'is a large place, Cebes, and has many good men, and there are barbarous races not a few: seek for him among them all, far and wide, sparing neither pains nor money; for there is no better way of using your money. And you must not forget to seek for him among yourselves too; for he is nowhere more likely to be found.'

'The search,' replied Cebes, 'shall certainly be made. And now, if you please, let us return to the point of the argument at which we digressed.'

'By all means,' replied Socrates; 'what else should I please?'

'Very good,' he said.

'Must we not,' said Socrates, 'ask ourselves some question of this sort? – What is that which, as we imagine, is liable to be scattered away, and about which we fear? and what again is that about which we have no fear? And then we may proceed to inquire whether that which suffers dispersion is or is not of the nature of soul – our hopes and fears as to our own souls will turn upon that.'

'That is true,' he said.

'Now the compound or composite may be supposed to be naturally capable of being dissolved in like manner as of being compounded; but that which is uncompounded, and that only, must be, if anything is, indissoluble.'

'Yes; that is what I should imagine,' said Cebes.

'And the uncompounded may be assumed to be the same and unchanging, where the compound is always changing and never the same?'

'That I also think,' he said.

'Then now let us return to the previous discussion. Is that idea or essence, which in the dialectical process we define as essence of true existence – whether essence of equality, beauty, or anything else: are these essences, I say, liable at times to some degree of change? Or are they each of them always what they are, having the same simple, self-existent and unchanging forms, and not admitting of variation at all, or in any way, or at any time?'

'They must be always the same, Socrates,' replied Cebes.

'And what would you say of the many beautiful – whether men or horses or garments or any other things which may be called equal or beautiful – are they all unchanging and the same always, or quite the reverse? May they not rather be described as almost always changing and hardly ever the same either with themselves or with one another?'

'The latter,' replied Cebes; 'they are always in a state of change.'

'And these you can touch and see and perceive with the senses, but the unchanging things you can only perceive with the mind – they are invisible and are not seen?'

'That is very true,' he said.

'Well, then,' he added, 'let us suppose that there are two sorts of existences, one seen, the other unseen.'

'Let us suppose them.'

'The seen is the changing, and the unseen is the unchanging.'

'That may be also supposed.'

'And, further, is not one part of us body, and the rest of us soul?'

'To be sure.'

'And to which class may we say that the body is more alike and akin?'

'Clearly to the seen: no one can doubt that.'

'And is the soul seen or not seen?'

'Not by man, Socrates.'

'And by "seen" and "not seen" is meant by us that which is or is not visible to the eye of man?'

'Yes, to the eye of man.'

'And what do we say of the soul? is that seen or not seen?'

'Not seen.'

'Unseen then?'

'Yes.'

'Then the soul is more like to the unseen, and the body to the seen?'

'That is most certain, Socrates.'

'And were we not saying long ago that the soul when using the body as an instrument of perception, that is to say, when using the sense of sight or hearing or some other sense (for the meaning of perceiving through the body is perceiving through the senses) – were we not saying that the soul too is then dragged by the body into the region of the changeable, and wanders and is confused; the world spins round her, and she is like a drunkard when under their influence?'

'Very true.'

'But when returning into herself she reflects; then she passes into the realm of purity, and eternity, and immortality, and unchangeableness, which are her kindred, and with them she ever lives, when she is by herself and is not let or hindered; then she ceases from her erring ways, and being in communion with the unchanging is unchanging. And this state of the soul is called wisdom?'

'That is well and truly said, Socrates,' he replied.

'And to which class is the soul more nearly alike and akin, as far as may be inferred from this argument, as well as from the preceding one?'

'I think, Socrates, that, in the opinion of everyone who follows the argument, the soul will be infinitely more like the unchangeable

– even the most stupid person will not deny that.'

'And the body is more like the changing?'

'Yes.'

'Yet once more consider the matter in this light: When the soul and the body are united, then nature orders the soul to rule and govern, and the body to obey and serve. Now which of these two functions is akin to the divine? and which to the mortal? Does not the divine appear to you to be that which naturally orders and rules, and the mortal that which is subject and servant?'

'True.'

'And which does the soul resemble?'

'The soul resembles the divine and the body the mortal – there can be no doubt of that, Socrates.'

'Then reflect, Cebes: is not the conclusion of the whole matter this? – that the soul is in the very likeness of the divine, and immortal, and intelligible, and uniform, and indissoluble, and unchangeable; and the body is in the very likeness of the human, and mortal, and unintelligible, and multiform, and dissoluble, and changeable. Can this, my dear Cebes, be denied?'

'No, indeed.'

'But if this is true, then is not the body liable to speedy dissolution? and is not the soul almost or altogether indissoluble?'

'Certainly.'

'And do you further observe, that after a man is dead, the body, which is the visible part of man, and has a visible framework, which is called a corpse, and which would naturally be dissolved and decomposed and dissipated, is not dissolved or decomposed at once, but may remain for a good while, if the constitution be sound at the time of death, and the season of the year favourable? For the body when shrunk and embalmed, as is the custom in Egypt, may remain almost entire through infinite ages; and even in decay, still there are some portions, such as the bones and ligaments, which are practically indestructible. You allow that?'

'Yes.'

'And are we to suppose that the soul, which is invisible, in passing to the true Hades, which like her is invisible, and pure, and noble, and on her way to the good and wise God, whither, if God will, my soul is also soon to go – that the soul, I repeat, if this be her nature and origin, is blown away and perishes immediately on quitting the body as the many say? That can never be, dear Simmias and Cebes. The truth rather is that the soul which is pure at departing draws after her no bodily taint, having never voluntarily had connection with the body, which she is ever avoiding, herself gathered into herself (for such abstraction has been the study of her life). And what does this mean but that she has been a true disciple of philosophy and has practised how to die easily? And is not philosophy the practice of death?'

'Certainly.'

'That soul, I say, herself invisible, departs to the invisible world to the divine and immortal and rational: thither arriving, she lives in bliss and is released from the error and folly of men, their fears and wild passions and all other human ills, and forever dwells, as they say of the initiated, in company with the gods. Is not this true, Cebes?'

'Yes,' said Cebes, 'beyond a doubt.'

'But the soul which has been polluted, and is impure at the time of her departure, and is the companion and servant of the body always, and is in love with and fascinated by the body and by the desires and pleasures of the body, until she is led to believe that the truth only exists in a bodily form, which a man may touch and see and taste and use for the purposes of his lusts – the soul, I mean, accustomed to hate and fear and avoid the intellectual principle, which to the bodily eye is dark and invisible, and can be attained only by philosophy – do you suppose that such a soul as this will depart pure and unalloyed?'

'That is impossible,' he replied.

'She is engrossed by the corporeal, which the continual association and constant care of the body have made natural to her.'

'Very true.'

'And this, my friend, may be conceived to be that heavy, weighty, earthy element of sight by which such a soul is depressed and dragged down again into the visible world, because she is afraid of the invisible and of the world below – prowling about tombs and sepulchres, in the neighbourhood of which, as they tell us, are seen certain ghostly apparitions of souls which have not departed pure, but are cloyed with sight and therefore visible.'

'That is very likely, Socrates.'

'Yes, that is very likely, Cebes; and these must be the souls, not of the good, but of the evil, who are compelled to wander about such places in payment of the penalty of their former evil way of life; and they continue to wander until the desire which haunts them is satisfied and they are imprisoned in another body. And they may be supposed to be fixed in the same natures which they had in their former life.'

'What natures do you mean, Socrates?'

'I mean to say that men who have followed after gluttony, and wantonness, and drunkenness, and have had no thought of avoiding them, would pass into asses and animals of that sort. What do you think?'

'I think that exceedingly probable.'

'And those who have chosen the portion of injustice, and tyranny, and violence, will pass into wolves, or into hawks and kites; whither else can we suppose them to go?'

'Yes,' said Cebes; 'that is doubtless the place of natures such as theirs.'

'And there is no difficulty,' he said, 'in assigning to all of them places answering to their several natures and propensities?'

'There is not,' he said.

'Even among them some are happier than others; and the happiest both in themselves and their place of abode are those who have practised the civil and social virtues which are called temperance and justice, and are acquired by habit and attention

without philosophy and mind.'

'Why are they the happiest?'

'Because they may be expected to pass into some gentle, social nature which is like their own, such as that of bees or ants, or even back again into the form of man, and just and moderate men spring from them.'

'That is not impossible.'

'But he who is a philosopher or lover of learning, and is entirely pure at departing, is alone permitted to reach the gods. And this is the reason, Simmias and Cebes, why the true votaries of philosophy abstain from all fleshly lusts, and endure and refuse to give themselves up to them – not because they fear poverty or the ruin of their families, like the lovers of money, and the world in general; nor like the lovers of power and honor, because they dread the dishonour or disgrace of evil deeds.'

'No, Socrates, that would not become them,' said Cebes.

'No, indeed,' he replied; 'and therefore they who have a care of their souls, and do not merely live in the fashions of the body, say farewell to all this; they will not walk in the ways of the blind: and when philosophy offers them purification and release from evil, they feel that they ought not to resist her influence, and to her they incline, and whither she leads they follow her.'

'What do you mean, Socrates?'

'I will tell you,' he said. 'The lovers of knowledge are conscious that their souls, when philosophy receives them, are simply fastened and glued to their bodies: the soul is only able to view existence through the bars of a prison, and not in her own nature; she is wallowing in the mire of all ignorance; and philosophy, seeing the terrible nature of her confinement, and that the captive through desire is led to conspire in her own captivity (for the lovers of knowledge are aware that this was the original state of the soul, and that when she was in this state philosophy received and gently counselled her, and wanted to release her, pointing out to her that the eye is full of deceit, and also the ear and other senses, and

persuading her to retire from them in all but the necessary use of them and to be gathered up and collected into herself, and to trust only to herself and her own intuitions of absolute existence, and mistrust that which comes to her through others and is subject to vicissitude) – philosophy shows her that this is visible and tangible, but that what she sees in her own nature is intellectual and invisible. And the soul of the true philosopher thinks that she ought not to resist this deliverance, and therefore abstains from pleasures and desires and pains and fears, as far as she is able; reflecting that when a man has great joys or sorrows or fears or desires he suffers from them, not the sort of evil which might be anticipated – as, for example, the loss of his health or property, which he has sacrificed to his lusts – but he has suffered an evil greater far, which is the greatest and worst of all evils, and one of which he never thinks.'

'And what is that, Socrates?' said Cebes.

'Why, this: When the feeling of pleasure or pain in the soul is most intense, all of us naturally suppose that the object of this intense feeling is then plainest and truest: but this is not the case.'

'Very true.'

'And this is the state in which the soul is most enthralled by the body.'

'How is that?'

'Why, because each pleasure and pain is a sort of nail which nails and rivets the soul to the body, and engrosses her and makes her believe that to be true which the body affirms to be true; and from agreeing with the body and having the same delights she is obliged to have the same habits and ways, and is not likely ever to be pure at her departure to the world below, but is always saturated with the body; so that she soon sinks into another body and there germinates and grows, and has therefore no part in the communion of the divine and pure and simple.'

'That is most true, Socrates,' answered Cebes.

'And this, Cebes, is the reason why the true lovers of knowledge are temperate and brave; and not for the reason which

the world gives.'

'Certainly not.'

'Certainly not! For not in that way does the soul of a philosopher reason; she will not ask philosophy to release her in order that when released she may deliver herself up again to the thraldom of pleasures and pains, doing a work only to be undone again, weaving instead of unweaving her Penelope's web. But she will make herself a calm of passion and follow Reason, and dwell in her, beholding the true and divine (which is not matter of opinion), and thence derive nourishment. Thus she seeks to live while she lives, and after death she hopes to go to her own kindred and to be freed from human ills. Never fear, Simmias and Cebes, that a soul which has been thus nurtured and has had these pursuits, will at her departure from the body be scattered and blown away by the winds and be nowhere and nothing.'

When Socrates had done speaking, for a considerable time there was silence; he himself and most of us appeared to be meditating on what had been said; only Cebes and Simmias spoke a few words to one another. And Socrates observing this asked them what they thought of the argument, and whether there was anything wanting? 'For,' said he, 'much is still open to suspicion and attack, if anyone were disposed to sift the matter thoroughly. If you are talking of something else I would rather not interrupt you, but if you are still doubtful about the argument do not hesitate to say exactly what you think, and let us have anything better which you can suggest; and if I am likely to be of any use, allow me to help you.'

Simmias said: 'I must confess, Socrates, that doubts did arise in our minds, and each of us was urging and inciting the other to put the question which he wanted to have answered and which neither of us liked to ask, fearing that our importunity might be troublesome under present circumstances.'

Socrates smiled and said: 'O Simmias, how strange that is; I am not very likely to persuade other men that I do not regard my present situation as a misfortune, if I am unable to persuade you,

and you will keep fancying that I am at all more troubled now than at any other time. Will you not allow that I have as much of the spirit of prophecy in me as the swans? For they, when they perceive that they must die, having sung all their life long, do then sing more than ever, rejoicing in the thought that they are about to go away to the god whose ministers they are. But men, because they are themselves afraid of death, slanderously affirm of the swans that they sing a lament at the last, not considering that no bird sings when cold, or hungry, or in pain, not even the nightingale, nor the swallow, nor yet the hoopoe; which are said indeed to tune a lay of sorrow, although I do not believe this to be true of them any more than of the swans. But because they are sacred to Apollo and have the gift of prophecy and anticipate the good things of another world, therefore they sing and rejoice in that day more than they ever did before. And I, too, believing myself to be the consecrated servant of the same God, and the fellow servant of the swans, and thinking that I have received from my master gifts of prophecy which are not inferior to theirs, would not go out of life less merrily than the swans. Cease to mind then about this, but speak and ask anything which you like, while the eleven magistrates of Athens allow.'

'Well, Socrates,' said Simmias, 'then I will tell you my difficulty, and Cebes will tell you his. For I dare say that you, Socrates, feel, as I do, how very hard or almost impossible is the attainment of any certainty about questions such as these in the present life. And yet I should deem him a coward who did not prove what is said about them to the uttermost, or whose heart failed him before he had examined them on every side. For he should persevere until he has attained one of two things: either he should discover or learn the truth about them; or, if this is impossible, I would have him take the best and most irrefragable of human notions, and let this be the raft upon which he sails through life – not without risk, as I admit, if he cannot find some word of God which will more surely and safely carry him. And now, as you bid me, I will venture to question you, as I should not like to reproach myself hereafter with not having said at the time what I think. For when I consider the matter either alone or with Cebes, the argument does certainly appear to me, Socrates, to be not sufficient.'

Socrates answered: 'I dare say, my friend, that you may be right, but I should like to know in what respect the argument is not sufficient.'

'In this respect,' replied Simmias, 'might not a person use the same argument about harmony and the lyre – might he not say that harmony is a thing invisible, incorporeal, fair, divine, abiding in the lyre which is harmonized, but that the lyre and the strings are matter and material, composite, earthy, and akin to mortality? And when someone breaks the lyre, or cuts and rends the strings, then he who takes this view would argue as you do, and on the same analogy, that the harmony survives and has not perished; for you cannot imagine, as we would say, that the lyre without the strings, and the broken strings themselves, remain, and yet that the harmony, which is of heavenly and immortal nature and kindred, has perished – and perished too before the mortal. The harmony, he would say, certainly exists somewhere, and the wood and strings will decay before that decays. For I suspect, Socrates, that the notion of the soul which we are all of us inclined to entertain, would also be yours, and that you too would conceive the body to be strung up, and held together, by the elements of hot and cold, wet and dry, and the like, and that the soul is the harmony or due proportionate admixture of them. And, if this is true, the inference clearly is that when the strings of the body are unduly loosened or overstrained through disorder or other injury, then the soul, though most divine, like other harmonies of music or of the works of art, of course perishes at once, although the material remains of the body may last for a considerable time, until they are either decayed or burnt. Now if anyone maintained that the soul, being the harmony of the elements of the body, first perishes in that which is called death, how shall we answer him?'

Socrates looked round at us as his manner was, and said, with

a smile: 'Simmias has reason on his side; and why does not some one of you who is abler than myself answer him? for there is force in his attack upon me. But perhaps, before we answer him, we had better also hear what Cebes has to say against the argument – this will give us time for reflection, and when both of them have spoken, we may either assent to them if their words appear to be in consonance with the truth, or if not, we may take up the other side, and argue with them. Please to tell me then, Cebes,' he said, 'what was the difficulty which troubled you?'

Cebes said: 'I will tell you. My feeling is that the argument is still in the same position, and open to the same objections which were urged before; for I am ready to admit that the existence of the soul before entering into the bodily form has been very ingeniously, and, as I may be allowed to say, quite sufficiently proven; but the existence of the soul after death is still, in my judgement, unproven. Now my objection is not the same as that of Simmias; for I am not disposed to deny that the soul is stronger and more lasting than the body, being of opinion that in all such respects the soul very far excels the body. Well, then, says the argument to me, why do you remain unconvinced? When you see that the weaker is still in existence after the man is dead, will you not admit that the more lasting must also survive during the same period of time? Now I, like Simmias, must employ a figure; and I shall ask you to consider whether the figure is to the point. The parallel which I will suppose is that of an old weaver, who dies, and after his death somebody says: He is not dead, he must be alive; and he appeals to the coat which he himself wove and wore, and which is still whole and undecayed. And then he proceeds to ask of someone who is incredulous, whether a man lasts longer, or the coat which is in use and wear; and when he is answered that a man lasts far longer, thinks that he has thus certainly demonstrated the survival of the man, who is the more lasting, because the less lasting remains. But that, Simmias, as I would beg you to observe, is not the truth; everyone sees that he who talks thus is talking nonsense. For the truth is that this weaver, having worn and woven many such coats, though he outlived several of them, was himself outlived by the last; but this is surely very far from proving that a man is slighter and weaker than a coat. Now the relation of the body to the soul may be expressed in a similar figure; for you may say with reason that the soul is lasting, and the body weak and short-lived in comparison. And every soul may be said to wear out many bodies, especially in the course of a long life. For if while the man is alive the body deliquesces and decays, and yet the soul always weaves her garment anew and repairs the waste, then of course, when the soul perishes, she must have on her last garment, and this only will survive her; but then again when the soul is dead the body will at last show its native weakness, and soon pass into decay. And therefore this is an argument on which I would rather not rely as proving that the soul exists after death. For suppose that we grant even more than you affirm as within the range of possibility, and besides acknowledging that the soul existed before birth admit also that after death the souls of some are existing still, and will exist, and will be born and die again and again, and that there is a natural strength in the soul which will hold out and be born many times – for all this, we may be still inclined to think that she will weary in the labours of successive births, and may at last succumb in one of her deaths and utterly perish; and this death and dissolution of the body which brings destruction to the soul may be unknown to any of us, for no one of us can have had any experience of it: and if this be true, then I say that he who is confident in death has but a foolish confidence, unless he is able to prove that the soul is altogether immortal and imperishable. But if he is not able to prove this, he who is about to die will always have reason to fear that when the body is disunited, the soul also may utterly perish.'

All of us, as we afterwards remarked to one another, had an unpleasant feeling at hearing them say this. When we had been so firmly convinced before, now to have our faith shaken seemed to introduce a confusion and uncertainty, not only into the previous

argument, but into any future one; either we were not good judges, or there were no real grounds of belief.

ECH. There I feel with you – indeed I do, Phaedo, and when you were speaking, I was beginning to ask myself the same question: What argument can I ever trust again? For what could be more convincing than the argument of Socrates, which has now fallen into discredit? That the soul is a harmony is a doctrine which has always had a wonderful attraction for me, and, when mentioned, came back to me at once, as my own original conviction. And now I must begin again and find another argument which will assure me that when the man is dead the soul dies not with him. Tell me, I beg, how did Socrates proceed? Did he appear to share the unpleasant feeling which you mention? or did he receive the interruption calmly and give a sufficient answer? Tell us, as exactly as you can, what passed.

PHAED. Often, Echecrates, as I have admired Socrates, I never admired him more than at that moment. That he should be able to answer was nothing, but what astonished me was, first, the gentle and pleasant and approving manner in which he regarded the words of the young men, and then his quick sense of the wound which had been inflicted by the argument, and his ready application of the healing art. He might be compared to a general rallying his defeated and broken army, urging them to follow him and return to the field of argument.

ECH. How was that?

PHAED. You shall hear, for I was close to him on his right hand, seated on a sort of stool, and he on a couch which was a good deal higher. Now he had a way of playing with my hair, and then he smoothed my head, and pressed the hair upon my neck, and said: 'To-morrow, Phaedo, I suppose that these fair locks of yours will be severed.'

'Yes, Socrates, I suppose that they will,' I replied.

'Not so if you will take my advice.'

'What shall I do with them?' I said.

'To-day,' he replied, 'and not to-morrow, if this argument dies and cannot be brought to life again by us, you and I will both shave our locks; and if I were you, and could not maintain my ground against Simmias and Cebes, I would myself take an oath, like the Argives, not to wear hair any more until I had renewed the conflict and defeated them.'

'Yes,' I said, 'but Heracles himself is said not to be a match for two.'

'Summon me then,' he said, 'and I will be your Iolaus until the sun goes down.'

'I summon you rather,' I said, 'not as Heracles summoning Iolaus, but as Iolaus might summon Heracles.'

'That will be all the same,' he said. 'But first let us take care that we avoid a danger.'

'And what is that?' I said.

'The danger of becoming misologists,' he replied, 'which is one of the very worst things that can happen to us. For as there are misanthropists or haters of men, there are also misologists or haters of ideas, and both spring from the same cause, which is ignorance of the world. Misanthropy arises from the too great confidence of inexperience; you trust a man and think him altogether true and good and faithful, and then in a little while he turns out to be false and knavish; and then another and another, and when this has happened several times to a man, especially within the circle of his most trusted friends, as he deems them, and he has often quarrelled with them, he at last hates all men, and believes that no one has any good in him at all. I dare say that you must have observed this.'

'Yes,' I said.

'And is not this discreditable? The reason is that a man, having to deal with other men, has no knowledge of them; for if he had knowledge he would have known the true state of the case, that few are the good and few the evil, and that the great majority are in the interval between them.'

'How do you mean?' I said.

'I mean,' he replied, 'as you might say of the very large and very small, that nothing is more uncommon than a very large or a very small man; and this applies generally to all extremes, whether of great and small, or swift and slow, or fair and foul, or black and white: and whether the instances you select be men or dogs or anything else, few are the extremes, but many are in the mean between them. Did you never observe this?'

'Yes,' I said, 'I have.'

'And do you not imagine,' he said, 'that if there were a competition of evil, the first in evil would be found to be very few?'

'Yes, that is very likely,' I said.

'Yes, that is very likely,' he replied; 'not that in this respect arguments are like men – there I was led on by you to say more than I had intended; but the point of comparison was that when a simple man who has no skill in dialectics believes an argument to be true which he afterwards imagines to be false, whether really false or not, and then another and another, he has no longer any faith left, and great disputers, as you know, come to think at last that they have grown to be the wisest of mankind; for they alone perceive the utter unsoundness and instability of all arguments, or, indeed, of all things, which, like the currents in the Euripus, are going up and down in never-ceasing ebb and flow.'

'That is quite true,' I said.

'Yes, Phaedo,' he replied, 'and very melancholy too, if there be such a thing as truth or certainty or power of knowing at all, that a man should have lighted upon some argument or other which at first seemed true and then turned out to be false, and instead of blaming himself and his own want of wit, because he is annoyed, should at last be too glad to transfer the blame from himself to arguments in general; and forever afterwards should hate and revile them, and lose the truth and knowledge of existence.'

'Yes, indeed,' I said; 'that is very melancholy.'

'Let us, then, in the first place,' he said, 'be careful of admitting into our souls the notion that there is no truth or health or

soundness in any arguments at all; but let us rather say that there is as yet no health in us, and that we must quit ourselves like men and do our best to gain health – you and all other men with a view to the whole of your future life, and I myself with a view to death. For at this moment I am sensible that I have not the temper of a philosopher; like the vulgar, I am only a partisan. For the partisan, when he is engaged in a dispute, cares nothing about the rights of the question, but is anxious only to convince his hearers of his own assertions. And the difference between him and me at the present moment is only this – that whereas he seeks to convince his hearers that what he says is true, I am rather seeking to convince myself; to convince my hearers is a secondary matter with me. And do but see how much I gain by this. For if what I say is true, then I do well to be persuaded of the truth, but if there be nothing after death, still, during the short time that remains, I shall save my friends from lamentations, and my ignorance will not last, and therefore no harm will be done. This is the state of mind, Simmias and Cebes, in which I approach the argument. And I would ask you to be thinking of the truth and not of Socrates: agree with me, if I seem to you to be speaking the truth; or if not, withstand me might and main, that I may not deceive you as well as myself in my enthusiasm, and, like the bee, leave my sting in you before I die.'

'And now let us proceed,' he said. 'And first of all let me be sure that I have in my mind what you were saying. Simmias, if I remember rightly, has fears and misgivings whether the soul, being in the form of harmony, although a fairer and diviner thing than the body, may not perish first. On the other hand, Cebes appeared to grant that the soul was more lasting than the body, but he said that no one could know whether the soul, after having worn out many bodies, might not perish herself and leave her last body behind her; and that this is death, which is the destruction not of the body but of the soul, for in the body the work of destruction is ever going on. Are not these, Simmias and Cebes, the points which we have to consider?'

They both agreed to this statement of them.

He proceeded: 'And did you deny the force of the whole preceding argument, or of a part only?'

'Of a part only,' they replied.

'And what did you think,' he said, 'of that part of the argument in which we said that knowledge was recollection only, and inferred from this that the soul must have previously existed somewhere else before she was enclosed in the body?'

Cebes said that he had been wonderfully impressed by that part of the argument, and that his conviction remained unshaken. Simmias agreed, and added that he himself could hardly imagine the possibility of his ever thinking differently about that.

'But,' rejoined Socrates, 'you will have to think differently, my Theban friend, if you still maintain that harmony is a compound, and that the soul is a harmony which is made out of strings set in the frame of the body; for you will surely never allow yourself to say that a harmony is prior to the elements which compose the harmony.'

'No, Socrates, that is impossible.'

'But do you not see that you are saying this when you say that the soul existed before she took the form and body of man, and was made up of elements which as yet had no existence? For harmony is not a sort of thing like the soul, as you suppose; but first the lyre, and the strings, and the sounds exist in a state of discord, and then harmony is made last of all, and perishes first. And how can such a notion of the soul as this agree with the other?'

'Not at all,' replied Simmias.

'And yet,' he said, 'there surely ought to be harmony when harmony is the theme of discourse.'

'There ought,' replied Simmias.

'But there is no harmony,' he said, 'in the two propositions that knowledge is recollection, and that the soul is a harmony. Which of them, then, will you retain?'

'I think,' he replied, 'that I have a much stronger faith, Socrates,

PHAEDO

in the first of the two, which has been fully demonstrated to me, than in the latter, which has not been demonstrated at all, but rests only on probable and plausible grounds; and I know too well that these arguments from probabilities are impostors, and unless great caution is observed in the use of them they are apt to be deceptive – in geometry, and in other things too. But the doctrine of knowledge and recollection has been proven to me on trustworthy grounds; and the proof was that the soul must have existed before she came into the body, because to her belongs the essence of which the very name implies existence. Having, as I am convinced, rightly accepted this conclusion, and on sufficient grounds, I must, as I suppose, cease to argue or allow others to argue that the soul is a harmony.'

'Let me put the matter, Simmias,' he said, 'in another point of view: Do you imagine that a harmony or any other composition can be in a state other than that of the elements out of which it is compounded?'

'Certainly not.'

'Or do or suffer anything other than they do or suffer?'

He agreed.

'Then a harmony does not lead the parts or elements which make up the harmony, but only follows them.'

He assented.

'For harmony cannot possibly have any motion, or sound, or other quality which is opposed to the parts.'

'That would be impossible,' he replied.

'And does not every harmony depend upon the manner in which the elements are harmonized?'

'I do not understand you,' he said.

'I mean to say that a harmony admits of degrees, and is more of a harmony, and more completely a harmony, when more completely harmonized, if that be possible; and less of a harmony, and less completely a harmony, when less harmonized.'

'True.'

'But does the soul admit of degrees? or is one soul in the very

least degree more or less, or more or less completely, a soul than another?'

'Not in the least.'

'Yet surely one soul is said to have intelligence and virtue, and to be good, and another soul is said to have folly and vice, and to be an evil soul: and this is said truly?'

'Yes, truly.'

'But what will those who maintain the soul to be a harmony say of this presence of virtue and vice in the soul? – Will they say that there is another harmony, and another discord, and that the virtuous soul is harmonized, and herself being a harmony has another harmony within her, and that the vicious soul is inharmonical and has no harmony within her?'

'I cannot say,' replied Simmias; 'but I suppose that something of that kind would be asserted by those who take this view.'

'And the admission is already made that no soul is more a soul than another; and this is equivalent to admitting that harmony is not more or less harmony, or more or less completely a harmony?'

'Quite true.'

'And that which is not more or less a harmony is not more or less harmonized?'

'True.'

'And that which is not more or less harmonized cannot have more or less of harmony, but only an equal harmony?'

'Yes, an equal harmony.'

'Then one soul not being more or less absolutely a soul than another, is not more or less harmonized?'

'Exactly.'

'And therefore has neither more nor less of harmony or of discord?'

'She has not.'

'And having neither more nor less of harmony or of discord, one soul has no more vice or virtue than another, if vice be discord and virtue harmony?'

'Not at all more.'

'Or speaking more correctly, Simmias, the soul, if she is a harmony, will never have any vice; because a harmony, being absolutely a harmony, has no part in the inharmonical?'

'No.'

'And therefore a soul which is absolutely a soul has no vice?'

'How can she have, consistently with the preceding argument?'

'Then, according to this, if the souls of all animals are equally and absolutely souls, they will be equally good?'

'I agree with you, Socrates,' he said.

'And can all this be true, think you?' he said; 'and are all these consequences admissible – which nevertheless seem to follow from the assumption that the soul is a harmony?'

'Certainly not,' he said.

'Once more,' he said, 'what ruling principle is there of human things other than the soul, and especially the wise soul? Do you know of any?'

'Indeed, I do not.'

'And is the soul in agreement with the affections of the body? Or is she at variance with them? For example, when the body is hot and thirsty, does not the soul incline us against drinking? and when the body is hungry, against eating? And this is only one instance out of ten thousand of the opposition of the soul to the things of the body.'

'Very true.'

'But we have already acknowledged that the soul, being a harmony, can never utter a note at variance with the tensions and relaxations and vibrations and other affections of the strings out of which she is composed; she can only follow, she cannot lead them?'

'Yes,' he said, 'we acknowledged that, certainly.'

'And yet do we not now discover the soul to be doing the exact opposite – leading the elements of which she is believed to be composed; almost always opposing and coercing them in all sorts of ways throughout life, sometimes more violently with the pains of

medicine and gymnastic; then again more gently; threatening and also reprimanding the desires, passions, fears, as if talking to a thing which is not herself, as Homer in the "Odyssey" represents Odysseus doing in the words:–

"He beat his breast, and thus reproached his heart:
endure, my heart; far worse hast thou endured!"

'Do you think that Homer could have written this under the idea that the soul is a harmony capable of being led by the affections of the body, and not rather of a nature which leads and masters them; and herself a far diviner thing than any harmony?'

'Yes, Socrates, I quite agree to that.'

'Then, my friend, we can never be right in saying that the soul is a harmony, for that would clearly contradict the divine Homer as well as ourselves.'

'True,' he said.

'Thus much,' said Socrates, 'of Harmonia, your Theban goddess, Cebes, who has not been ungracious to us, I think; but what shall I say to the Theban Cadmus, and how shall I propitiate him?'

'I think that you will discover a way of propitiating him,' said Cebes; 'I am sure that you have answered the argument about harmony in a manner that I could never have expected. For when Simmias mentioned his objection, I quite imagined that no answer could be given to him, and therefore I was surprised at finding that his argument could not sustain the first onset of yours; and not impossibly the other, whom you call Cadmus, may share a similar fate.'

'Nay, my good friend,' said Socrates, 'let us not boast, lest some evil eye should put to flight the word which I am about to speak. That, however, may be left in the hands of those above, while I draw near in Homeric fashion, and try the mettle of your words. Briefly, the sum of your objection is as follows: You want to have proven to you that the soul is imperishable and immortal, and you think that the philosopher who is confident in death has but a vain and foolish confidence, if he thinks that he will fare better than one

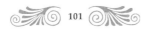

who has led another sort of life, in the world below, unless he can prove this; and you say that the demonstration of the strength and divinity of the soul, and of her existence prior to our becoming men, does not necessarily imply her immortality. Granting that the soul is long-lived, and has known and done much in a former state, still she is not on that account immortal; and her entrance into the human form may be a sort of disease which is the beginning of dissolution, and may at last, after the toils of life are over, end in that which is called death. And whether the soul enters into the body once only or many times, that, as you would say, makes no difference in the fears of individuals. For any man, who is not devoid of natural feeling, has reason to fear, if he has no knowledge or proof of the soul's immortality. That is what I suppose you to say, Cebes, which I designedly repeat, in order that nothing may escape us, and that you may, if you wish, add or subtract anything.'

'But,' said Cebes, 'as far as I can see at present, I have nothing to add or subtract; you have expressed my meaning.'

Socrates paused awhile, and seemed to be absorbed in reflection. At length he said: 'This is a very serious inquiry which you are raising, Cebes, involving the whole question of generation and corruption, about which I will, if you like, give you my own experience; and you can apply this, if you think that anything which I say will avail towards the solution of your difficulty.'

'I should very much like,' said Cebes, 'to hear what you have to say.'

'Then I will tell you,' said Socrates. 'When I was young, Cebes, I had a prodigious desire to know that department of philosophy which is called Natural Science; this appeared to me to have lofty aims, as being the science which has to do with the causes of things, and which teaches why a thing is, and is created and destroyed; and I was always agitating myself with the consideration of such questions as these: Is the growth of animals the result of some decay which the hot and cold principle contracts, as some have said? Is the blood the element with which we think, or the air, or the fire? or perhaps nothing of this sort – but the brain may be the originating power of the perceptions of hearing and sight and smell, and memory and opinion may come from them, and science may be based on memory and opinion when no longer in motion, but at rest. And then I went on to examine the decay of them, and then to the things of heaven and earth, and at last I concluded that I was wholly incapable of these inquiries, as I will satisfactorily prove to you. For I was fascinated by them to such a degree that my eyes grew blind to things that I had seemed to myself, and also to others, to know quite well; and I forgot what I had before thought to be self-evident, that the growth of man is the result of eating and drinking; for when by the digestion of food flesh is added to flesh and bone to bone, and whenever there is an aggregation of congenial elements, the lesser bulk becomes larger and the small man greater. Was not that a reasonable notion?'

'Yes,' said Cebes, 'I think so.'

'Well; but let me tell you something more. There was a time when I thought that I understood the meaning of greater and less pretty well; and when I saw a great man standing by a little one I fancied that one was taller than the other by a head; or one horse would appear to be greater than another horse: and still more clearly did I seem to perceive that ten is two more than eight, and that two cubits are more than one, because two is twice one.'

'And what is now your notion of such matters?' said Cebes.

'I should be far enough from imagining,' he replied, 'that I knew the cause of any of them, indeed I should, for I cannot satisfy myself that when one is added to one, the one to which the addition is made becomes two, or that the two units added together make two by reason of the addition. For I cannot understand how, when separated from the other, each of them was one and not two, and now, when they are brought together, the mere juxtaposition of them can be the cause of their becoming two: nor can I understand how the division of one is the way to make two; for then a different cause would produce the same effect – as in the former instance the addition and juxtaposition of one to one was the cause of two, in this the separation and subtraction of one from the other would be the cause. Nor am I any longer satisfied that I understand the reason why one or anything else either is generated or destroyed or is at all, but I have in my mind some confused notion of another method, and can never admit this.

'Then I heard someone who had a book of Anaxagoras, as he said, out of which he read that mind was the disposer and cause of all, and I was quite delighted at the notion of this, which appeared admirable, and I said to myself: If mind is the disposer, mind will dispose all for the best, and put each particular in the best place; and I argued that if anyone desired to find out the cause of the generation or destruction or existence of anything, he must find out what state of being or suffering or doing was best for that thing, and therefore a man had only to consider the best for himself and others, and then he would also know the worse, for that the same science comprised both. And I rejoiced to think that I had found in Anaxagoras a teacher of the causes of existence such as I desired, and I imagined that he would tell me first whether the earth is flat or round; and then he would further explain the cause and the necessity of this, and would teach me the nature of the best and show that this was best; and if he said that the earth was in the centre, he would explain that this position was the best, and I should be satisfied if this were shown to me, and not want any other sort of cause. And I thought that I would then go and ask him about the sun and moon and stars, and that he would explain to me their comparative swiftness, and their returnings and various states, and how their several affections, active and passive, were all for the best. For I could not imagine that when he spoke of mind as the

disposer of them, he would give any other account of their being as they are, except that this was best; and I thought when he had explained to me in detail the cause of each and the cause of all, he would go on to explain to me what was best for each and what was best for all. I had hopes which I would not have sold for much, and I seized the books and read them as fast as I could in my eagerness to know the better and the worse.

'What hopes I had formed, and how grievously was I disappointed! As I proceeded, I found my philosopher altogether forsaking mind or any other principle of order, but having recourse to air, and ether, and water, and other eccentricities. I might compare him to a person who began by maintaining generally that mind is the cause of the actions of Socrates, but who, when he endeavoured to explain the causes of my several actions in detail, went on to show that I sit here because my body is made up of bones and muscles; and the bones, as he would say, are hard and have ligaments which divide them, and the muscles are elastic, and they cover the bones, which have also a covering or environment of flesh and skin which contains them; and as the bones are lifted at their joints by the contraction or relaxation of the muscles, I am able to bend my limbs, and this is why I am sitting here in a curved posture: that is what he would say, and he would have a similar explanation of my talking to you, which he would attribute to sound, and air, and hearing, and he would assign ten thousand other causes of the same sort, forgetting to mention the true cause, which is that the Athenians have thought fit to condemn me, and accordingly I have thought it better and more right to remain here and undergo my sentence; for I am inclined to think that these muscles and bones of mine would have gone off to Megara or Boeotia – by the dog of Egypt they would, if they had been guided only by their own idea of what was best, and if I had not chosen as the better and nobler part, instead of playing truant and running away, to undergo any punishment which the State inflicts. There is surely a strange confusion of causes and conditions in all this. It may be said, indeed, that without bones and muscles and the other parts of the body I cannot execute my purposes. But to say that I do as I do because of them, and that this is the way in which mind acts, and not from the choice of the best, is a very careless and idle mode of speaking. I wonder that they cannot distinguish the cause from the condition, which the many, feeling about in the dark, are always mistaking and misnaming. And thus one man makes a vortex all round and steadies the earth by the heaven; another gives the air as a support to the earth, which is a sort of broad trough. Any power which in disposing them as they are disposes them for the best never enters into their minds, nor do they imagine that there is any superhuman strength in that; they rather expect to find another Atlas of the world who is stronger and more everlasting and more containing than the good is, and are clearly of opinion that the obligatory and containing power of the good is as nothing; and yet this is the principle which I would fain learn if anyone would teach me. But as I have failed either to discover myself or to learn of anyone else, the nature of the best, I will exhibit to you, if you like, what I have found to be the second best mode of inquiring into the cause.'

'I should very much like to hear that,' he replied.

Socrates proceeded: 'I thought that as I had failed in the contemplation of true existence, I ought to be careful that I did not lose the eye of my soul; as people may injure their bodily eye by observing and gazing on the sun during an eclipse, unless they take the precaution of only looking at the image reflected in the water, or in some similar medium. That occurred to me, and I was afraid that my soul might be blinded altogether if I looked at things with my eyes or tried by the help of the senses to apprehend them. And I thought that I had better have recourse to ideas, and seek in them the truth of existence. I dare say that the simile is not perfect – for I am very far from admitting that he who contemplates existence through the medium of ideas, sees them only "through a glass darkly," any more than he who sees them in their working and effects. However, this was the method which I adopted: I first assumed some principle which I judged to be the strongest, and then I affirmed as true whatever seemed to agree with this, whether relating to the cause or to anything else; and that which disagreed I regarded as untrue. But I should like to explain my meaning clearly, as I do not think that you understand me.'

'No, indeed,' replied Cebes, 'not very well.'

'There is nothing new,' he said, 'in what I am about to tell you; but only what I have been always and everywhere repeating in the previous discussion and on other occasions: I want to show you the nature of that cause which has occupied my thoughts, and I shall have to go back to those familiar words which are in the mouth of everyone, and first of all assume that there is an absolute beauty and goodness and greatness, and the like; grant me this, and I hope to be able to show you the nature of the cause, and to prove the immortality of the soul.'

Cebes said: 'You may proceed at once with the proof, as I readily grant you this.'

'Well,' he said, 'then I should like to know whether you agree with me in the next step; for I cannot help thinking that if there be anything beautiful other than absolute beauty, that can only be beautiful in as far as it partakes of absolute beauty – and this I should say of everything. Do you agree in this notion of the cause?'

'Yes,' he said, 'I agree.'

He proceeded: 'I know nothing and can understand nothing of any other of those wise causes which are alleged; and if a person says to me that the bloom of colour, or form, or anything else of that sort is a source of beauty, I leave all that, which is only confusing to me, and simply and singly, and perhaps foolishly, hold and am assured in my own mind that nothing makes a thing beautiful but the presence and participation of beauty in whatever way or manner obtained; for as to the manner I am uncertain, but I stoutly contend that by beauty all beautiful things become beautiful. That appears to me to be the only safe answer that I can give, either to myself or to any other, and to that I cling, in the persuasion that I shall never be overthrown, and that I may safely answer to myself or any other that by beauty beautiful things become beautiful. Do you not agree to that?'

'Yes, I agree.'

'And that by greatness only great things become great and greater, greater, and by smallness the less becomes less.'

'True.'

'Then if a person remarks that A is taller by a head than B, and B less by a head than A, you would refuse to admit this, and would stoutly contend that what you mean is only that the greater is greater by, and by reason of, greatness, and the less is less only by, or by reason of, smallness; and thus you would avoid the danger of saying that the greater is greater and the less by the measure of the head, which is the same in both, and would also avoid the monstrous absurdity of supposing that the greater man is greater by reason of the head, which is small. Would you not be afraid of that?'

'Indeed, I should,' said Cebes, laughing.

'In like manner you would be afraid to say that ten exceeded eight by, and by reason of, two; but would say by, and by reason of, number; or that two cubits exceed one cubit not by a half, but by magnitude? – that is what you would say, for there is the same danger in both cases.'

'Very true,' he said.

'Again, would you not be cautious of affirming that the addition of one to one, or the division of one, is the cause of two? And you would loudly asseverate that you know of no way in which anything comes into existence except by participation in its own proper essence, and consequently, as far as you know, the only cause of two is the participation in duality; that is the way to make two, and the participation in one is the way to make one. You would say: I will let alone puzzles of division and addition – wiser heads than mine may answer them; inexperienced as I am, and ready to start, as the proverb says, at my own shadow, I cannot afford to give up the sure ground of a principle. And if anyone assails you there, you would not mind him, or answer him until you had seen whether the consequences which follow agree with one another or not, and when you are further required to give an explanation of this principle, you would go on to assume a higher principle, and the best of the higher ones, until you found a resting-place; but you would not refuse the principle and the consequences in your reasoning like the Eristics – at least if you wanted to discover real existence. Not that this confusion signifies to them who never care or think about the matter at all, for they have the wit to be well pleased with themselves, however great may be the turmoil of their ideas. But you, if you are a philosopher, will, I believe, do as I say.'

'What you say is most true,' said Simmias and Cebes, both speaking at once.

ECH. Yes, Phaedo; and I don't wonder at their assenting. Anyone who has the least sense will acknowledge the wonderful clearness of Socrates' reasoning.

PHAED. Certainly, Echecrates; and that was the feeling of the whole company at the time.

ECH. Yes, and equally of ourselves, who were not of the company, and are now listening to your recital. But what followed?

PHAEDO. After all this was admitted, and they had agreed about the existence of ideas and the participation in them of the other things which derive their names from them, Socrates, if I remember rightly, said: 'This is your way of speaking; and yet when you say that Simmias is greater than Socrates and less than Phaedo, do you not predicate of Simmias both greatness and smallness?'

'Yes, I do.'

'But still you allow that Simmias does not really exceed Socrates, as the words may seem to imply, because he is Simmias, but by reason of the size which he has; just as Simmias does not exceed Socrates because he is Simmias, any more than because Socrates is Socrates, but because he has smallness when compared with the greatness of Simmias?'

'True.'

'And if Phaedo exceeds him in size, that is not because Phaedo is Phaedo, but because Phaedo has greatness relatively to Simmias, who is comparatively smaller?'

'That is true.'

'And therefore Simmias is said to be great, and is also said to be small, because he is in a mean between them, exceeding the smallness of the one by his greatness, and allowing the greatness of the other to exceed his smallness.' He added, laughing, 'I am speaking like a book, but I believe that what I am now saying is true.'

Simmias assented to this.

'The reason why I say this is that I want you to agree with me in thinking, not only that absolute greatness will never be great and also small, but that greatness in us or in the concrete will never admit the small or admit of being exceeded: instead of this, one of two things will happen – either the greater will fly or retire before the opposite, which is the less, or at the advance of the less will cease to exist; but will not, if allowing or admitting smallness, be changed by that; even as I, having received and admitted smallness when compared with Simmias, remain just as I was, and am the same small person. And as the idea of greatness cannot condescend ever to be or become small, in like manner the smallness in us cannot be or become great; nor can any other opposite which remains the same ever be or become its own opposite, but either passes away or perishes in the change.'

'That,' replied Cebes, 'is quite my notion.'

One of the company, though I do not exactly remember which of them, on hearing this, said: 'By Heaven, is not this the direct contrary of what was admitted before – that out of the greater came the less and out of the less the greater, and that opposites are simply generated from opposites; whereas now this seems to be utterly denied.'

Socrates inclined his head to the speaker and listened. 'I like your courage,' he said, 'in reminding us of this. But you do not

observe that there is a difference in the two cases. For then we were speaking of opposites in the concrete, and now of the essential opposite which, as is affirmed, neither in us nor in nature can ever be at variance with itself: then, my friend, we were speaking of things in which opposites are inherent and which are called after them, but now about the opposites which are inherent in them and which give their name to them; these essential opposites will never, as we maintain, admit of generation into or out of one another.' At the same time, turning to Cebes, he said: 'Were you at all disconcerted, Cebes, at our friend's objection?'

'That was not my feeling,' said Cebes; 'and yet I cannot deny that I am apt to be disconcerted.'

'Then we are agreed after all,' said Socrates, 'that the opposite will never in any case be opposed to itself?'

'To that we are quite agreed,' he replied.

'Yet once more let me ask you to consider the question from another point of view, and see whether you agree with me: There is a thing which you term heat, and another thing which you term cold?'

'Certainly.'

'But are they the same as fire and snow?'

'Most assuredly not.'

'Heat is not the same as fire, nor is cold the same as snow?'

'No.'

'And yet you will surely admit that when snow, as before said, is under the influence of heat, they will not remain snow and heat; but at the advance of the heat the snow will either retire or perish?'

'Very true,' he replied.

'And the fire too at the advance of the cold will either retire or perish; and when the fire is under the influence of the cold, they will not remain, as before, fire and cold.'

'That is true,' he said.

'And in some cases the name of the idea is not confined to the idea; but anything else which, not being the idea, exists only in the

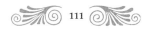

form of the idea, may also lay claim to it. I will try to make this clearer by an example: The odd number is always called by the name of odd?'

'Very true.'

'But is this the only thing which is called odd? Are there not other things which have their own name, and yet are called odd, because, although not the same as oddness, they are never without oddness? – that is what I mean to ask – whether numbers such as the number three are not of the class of odd. And there are many other examples: would you not say, for example, that three may be called by its proper name, and also be called odd, which is not the same with three? and this may be said not only of three but also of five, and every alternate number – each of them without being oddness is odd, and in the same way two and four, and the whole series of alternate numbers, has every number even, without being evenness. Do you admit that?'

'Yes,' he said, 'how can I deny that?'

'Then now mark the point at which I am aiming: not only do essential opposites exclude one another, but also concrete things, which, although not in themselves opposed, contain opposites; these, I say, also reject the idea which is opposed to that which is contained in them, and at the advance of that they either perish or withdraw. There is the number three for example; will not that endure annihilation or anything sooner than be converted into an even number, remaining three?'

'Very true,' said Cebes.

'And yet,' he said, 'the number two is certainly not opposed to the number three?'

'It is not.'

'Then not only do opposite ideas repel the advance of one another, but also there are other things which repel the approach of opposites.'

'That is quite true,' he said.

'Suppose,' he said, 'that we endeavour, if possible, to

determine what these are.'

'By all means.'

'Are they not, Cebes, such as compel the things of which they have possession, not only to take their own form, but also the form of some opposite?'

'What do you mean?'

'I mean, as I was just now saying, and have no need to repeat to you, that those things which are possessed by the number three must not only be three in number, but must also be odd.'

'Quite true.'

'And on this oddness, of which the number three has the impress, the opposite idea will never intrude?'

'No.'

'And this impress was given by the odd principle?'

'Yes.'

'And to the odd is opposed the even?'

'True.'

'Then the idea of the even number will never arrive at three?'

'No.'

'Then three has no part in the even?'

'None.'

'Then the triad or number three is uneven?'

'Very true.'

'To return then to my distinction of natures which are not opposites, and yet do not admit opposites: as, in this instance, three, although not opposed to the even, does not any the more admit of the even, but always brings the opposite into play on the other side; or as two does not receive the odd, or fire the cold – from these examples (and there are many more of them) perhaps you may be able to arrive at the general conclusion that not only opposites will not receive opposites, but also that nothing which brings the opposite will admit the opposite of that which it brings in that to which it is brought. And here let me recapitulate – for there is no harm in repetition. The number five will not admit the nature of the even, any more than ten, which is the double of five, will admit the nature of the odd – the double, though not strictly opposed to the odd, rejects the odd altogether. Nor again will parts in the ratio of 3:2, nor any fraction in which there is a half, nor again in which there is a third, admit the notion of the whole, although they are not opposed to the whole. You will agree to that?'

'Yes,' he said, 'I entirely agree and go along with you in that.'

'And now,' he said, 'I think that I may begin again; and to the question which I am about to ask I will beg you to give not the old safe answer, but another, of which I will offer you an example; and I hope that you will find in what has been just said another foundation which is as safe. I mean that if anyone asks you "what that is, the inherence of which makes the body hot," you will reply not heat (this is what I call the safe and stupid answer), but fire, a far better answer, which we are now in a condition to give. Or if anyone asks you "why a body is diseased," you will not say from disease, but from fever; and instead of saying that oddness is the cause of odd numbers, you will say that monad is the cause of them: and so of things in general, as I dare say that you will understand sufficiently without my adducing any further examples.'

'Yes,' he said, 'I quite understand you.'

'Tell me, then, what is that the inherence of which will render the body alive?'

'The soul,' he replied.

'And is this always the case?'

'Yes,' he said, 'of course.'

'Then whatever the soul possesses, to that she comes bearing life?'

'Yes, certainly.'

'And is there any opposite to life?'

'There is,' he said.

'And what is that?'

'Death.'

'Then the soul, as has been acknowledged, will never receive

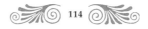

the opposite of what she brings. And now,' he said, 'what did we call that principle which repels the even?'

'The odd.'

'And that principle which repels the musical, or the just?'

'The unmusical,' he said, 'and the unjust.'

'And what do we call the principle which does not admit of death?'

'The immortal,' he said.

'And does the soul admit of death?'

'No.'

'Then the soul is immortal?'

'Yes,' he said.

'And may we say that this is proven?'

'Yes, abundantly proven, Socrates,' he replied.

'And supposing that the odd were imperishable, must not three be imperishable?'

'Of course.'

'And if that which is cold were imperishable, when the warm principle came attacking the snow, must not the snow have retired whole and unmelted – for it could never have perished, nor could it have remained and admitted the heat?'

'True,' he said.

'Again, if the uncooling or warm principle were imperishable, the fire when assailed by cold would not have perished or have been extinguished, but would have gone away unaffected?'

'Certainly,' he said.

'And the same may be said of the immortal: if the immortal is also imperishable, the soul when attacked by death cannot perish; for the preceding argument shows that the soul will not admit of death, or ever be dead, any more than three or the odd number will admit of the even, or fire or the heat in the fire, of the cold. Yet a person may say: "But although the odd will not become even at the approach of the even, why may not the odd perish and the even take the place of the odd?" Now to him who makes this objection, we cannot answer that the odd principle is imperishable; for this has not been acknowledged, but if this had been acknowledged, there would have been no difficulty in contending that at the approach of the even the odd principle and the number three took up their departure; and the same argument would have held good of fire and heat and any other thing.'

'Very true.'

'And the same may be said of the immortal: if the immortal is also imperishable, then the soul will be imperishable as well as immortal; but if not, some other proof of her imperishableness will have to be given.'

'No other proof is needed,' he said; 'for if the immortal, being eternal, is liable to perish, then nothing is imperishable.'

'Yes,' replied Socrates, 'all men will agree that God, and the essential form of life, and the immortal in general, will never perish.'

'Yes, all men,' he said; 'that is true; and what is more, gods, if I am not mistaken, as well as men.'

'Seeing then that the immortal is indestructible, must not the soul, if she is immortal, be also imperishable?'

'Most certainly.'

'Then when death attacks a man, the mortal portion of him may be supposed to die, but the immortal goes out of the way of death and is preserved safe and sound?'

'True.'

'Then, Cebes, beyond question the soul is immortal and imperishable, and our souls will truly exist in another world!'

'I am convinced, Socrates,' said Cebes, 'and have nothing more to object; but if my friend Simmias, or anyone else, has any further objection, he had better speak out, and not keep silence, since I do not know how there can ever be a more fitting time to which he can defer the discussion, if there is anything which he wants to say or have said.'

'But I have nothing more to say,' replied Simmias; 'nor do I see any room for uncertainty, except that which arises necessarily out of the greatness of the subject and the feebleness of man, and which I cannot help feeling.'

'Yes, Simmias,' replied Socrates, 'that is well said: and more than that, first principles, even if they appear certain, should be carefully considered; and when they are satisfactorily ascertained, then, with a sort of hesitating confidence in human reason, you may, I think, follow the course of the argument; and if this is clear, there will be no need for any further inquiry.'

'That,' he said, 'is true.'

'But then, O my friends,' he said, 'if the soul is really immortal, what care should be taken of her, not only in respect of the portion of time which is called life, but of eternity! And the danger of neglecting her from this point of view does indeed appear to be awful. If death had only been the end of all, the wicked would have had a good bargain in dying, for they would have been happily quit not only of their body, but of their own evil together with their souls. But now, as the soul plainly appears to be immortal, there is no release or salvation from evil except the attainment of the highest virtue and wisdom. For the soul when on her progress to the world below takes nothing with her but nurture and education; which are indeed said greatly to benefit or greatly to injure the departed, at the very beginning of its pilgrimage in the other world.

'For after death, as they say, the genius of each individual, to whom he belonged in life, leads him to a certain place in which the dead are gathered together for judgement, whence they go into the world below, following the guide who is appointed to conduct them from this world to the other: and when they have there received their due and remained their time, another guide brings them back again after many revolutions of ages. Now this journey to the other world is not, as Aeschylus says in the "Telephus," a single and straight path – no guide would be wanted for that, and no one could miss a single path; but there are many partings of the road, and windings, as I must infer from the rites and sacrifices which are offered to the gods below in places where three ways meet on earth. The wise and orderly soul is conscious of her situation and follows in the path; but the soul which desires the body, and which, as I was relating before, has long been fluttering about the lifeless frame and the world of sight, is after many struggles and many sufferings hardly and with violence carried away by her attendant genius, and when she arrives at the place where the other souls are gathered, if she be impure and have done impure deeds, or been concerned in foul murders or other crimes which are the brothers of these, and the works of brothers in crime – from that soul everyone flees and turns away; no one will be her companion, no one her guide, but alone she wanders in extremity of evil until certain times are fulfilled, and when they are fulfilled, she is borne irresistibly to her own fitting habitation; as every pure and just soul which has passed through life in the company and under the guidance of the gods has also her own proper home.

'Now the earth has divers wonderful regions, and is indeed in nature and extent very unlike the notions of geographers, as I believe on the authority of one who shall be nameless.'

'What do you mean, Socrates?' said Simmias. 'I have myself heard many descriptions of the earth, but I do not know in what you are putting your faith, and I should like to know.'

'Well, Simmias,' replied Socrates, 'the recital of a tale does not, I think, require the art of Glaucus; and I know not that the art of Glaucus could prove the truth of my tale, which I myself should never be able to prove, and even if I could, I fear, Simmias, that my life would come to an end before the argument was completed. I may describe to you, however, the form and regions of the earth according to my conception of them.'

'That,' said Simmias, 'will be enough.'

'Well, then,' he said, 'my conviction is that the earth is a round body in the centre of the heavens, and therefore has no need of air or any similar force as a support, but is kept there and hindered from falling or inclining any way by the equability of the surrounding heaven and by her own equipoise. For that which,

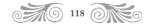

being in equipoise, is in the centre of that which is equably diffused, will not incline any way in any degree, but will always remain in the same state and not deviate. And this is my first notion.'

'Which is surely a correct one,' said Simmias.

'Also I believe that the earth is very vast, and that we who dwell in the region extending from the river Phasis to the Pillars of Heracles, along the borders of the sea, are just like ants or frogs about a marsh, and inhabit a small portion only, and that many others dwell in many like places. For I should say that in all parts of the earth there are hollows of various forms and sizes, into which the water and the mist and the air collect; and that the true earth is pure and in the pure heaven, in which also are the stars – that is the heaven which is commonly spoken of as the ether, of which this is but the sediment collecting in the hollows of the earth. But we who live in these hollows are deceived into the notion that we are dwelling above on the surface of the earth; which is just as if a creature who was at the bottom of the sea were to fancy that he was on the surface of the water, and that the sea was the heaven through which he saw the sun and the other stars – he having never come to the surface by reason of his feebleness and sluggishness, and having never lifted up his head and seen, nor ever heard from one who had seen, this region which is so much purer and fairer than his own. Now this is exactly our case: for we are dwelling in a hollow of the earth, and fancy that we are on the surface; and the air we call the heaven, and in this we imagine that the stars move. But this is also owing to our feebleness and sluggishness, which prevent our reaching the surface of the air: for if any man could arrive at the exterior limit, or take the wings of a bird and fly upward, like a fish who puts his head out and sees this world, he would see a world beyond; and, if the nature of man could sustain the sight, he would acknowledge that this was the place of the true heaven and the true light and the true stars. For this earth, and the stones, and the entire region which surrounds us, are spoilt and corroded, like the things in the sea which are corroded by the brine;

for in the sea too there is hardly any noble or perfect growth, but clefts only, and sand, and an endless slough of mud: and even the shore is not to be compared to the fairer sights of this world. And greater far is the superiority of the other. Now of that upper earth which is under the heaven, I can tell you a charming tale, Simmias, which is well worth hearing.'

'And we, Socrates,' replied Simmias, 'shall be charmed to listen.'

'The tale, my friend,' he said, 'is as follows: In the first place, the earth, when looked at from above, is like one of those balls which have leather coverings in twelve pieces, and is of divers colours, of which the colours which painters use on earth are only a sample. But there the whole earth is made up of them, and they are brighter far and clearer than ours; there is a purple of wonderful lustre, also the radiance of gold, and the white which is in the earth is whiter than any chalk or snow. Of these and other colours the earth is made up, and they are more in number and fairer than the eye of man has ever seen; and the very hollows (of which I was speaking) filled with air and water are seen like light flashing amid the other colours, and have a colour of their own, which gives a sort of unity to the variety of earth. And in this fair region everything that grows – trees, and flowers, and fruits – is in a like degree fairer than any here; and there are hills, and stones in them in a like degree smoother, and more transparent, and fairer in colour than our highly valued emeralds and sardonyxes and jaspers, and other gems, which are but minute fragments of them: for there all the stones are like our precious stones, and fairer still. The reason of this is that they are pure, and not, like our precious stones, infected or corroded by the corrupt briny elements which coagulate among us, and which breed foulness and disease both in earth and stones, as well as in animals and plants. They are the jewels of the upper earth, which also shines with gold and silver and the like, and they are visible to sight and large and abundant and found in every region of the earth, and blessed is he who sees them. And upon the earth are animals and men, some in a middle region, others dwelling about the air as we dwell about the sea; others in islands which the air flows round, near the continent: and in a word, the air is used by them as the water and the sea are by us, and the ether is to them what the air is to us. Moreover, the temperament of their seasons is such that they have no disease, and live much longer than we do, and have sight and hearing and smell, and all the other senses, in far greater perfection, in the same degree that air is purer than water or the ether than air. Also they have temples and sacred places in which the gods really dwell, and they hear their voices and receive their answers, and are conscious of them and hold converse with them, and they see the sun, moon, and stars as they really are, and their other blessedness is of a piece with this.

'Such is the nature of the whole earth, and of the things which are around the earth; and there are divers regions in the hollows on the face of the globe everywhere, some of them deeper and also wider than that which we inhabit, others deeper and with a narrower opening than ours, and some are shallower and wider; all have numerous perforations, and passages broad and narrow in the interior of the earth, connecting them with one another; and there flows into and out of them, as into basins, a vast tide of water, and huge subterranean streams of perennial rivers, and springs hot and cold, and a great fire, and great rivers of fire, and streams of liquid mud, thin or thick (like the rivers of mud in Sicily, and the lava-streams which follow them), and the regions about which they happen to flow are filled up with them. And there is a sort of swing in the interior of the earth which moves all this up and down. Now the swing is on this wise: There is a chasm which is the vastest of them all, and pierces right through the whole earth; this is that which Homer describes in the words,

"Far off, where is the inmost depth beneath the earth";

and which he in other places, and many other poets, have called Tartarus. And the swing is caused by the streams flowing into and out of this chasm, and they each have the nature of the soil through which they flow. And the reason why the streams are always

flowing in and out is that the watery element has no bed or bottom, and is surging and swinging up and down, and the surrounding wind and air do the same; they follow the water up and down, hither and thither, over the earth – just as in respiring the air is always in process of inhalation and exhalation; and the wind swinging with the water in and out produces fearful and irresistible blasts: when the waters retire with a rush into the lower parts of the earth, as they are called, they flow through the earth into those regions, and fill them up as with the alternate motion of a pump, and then when they leave those regions and rush back hither, they again fill the hollows here, and when these are filled, flow through subterranean channels and find their way to their several places, forming seas, and lakes, and rivers, and springs. Thence they again enter the earth, some of them making a long circuit into many lands, others going to few places and those not distant, and again fall into Tartarus, some at a point a good deal lower than that at which they rose, and others not much lower, but all in some degree lower than the point of issue. And some burst forth again on the opposite side, and some on the same side, and some wind round the earth with one or many folds, like the coils of a serpent, and descend as far as they can, but always return and fall into the lake. The rivers on either side can descend only to the centre and no further, for to the rivers on both sides the opposite side is a precipice.

'Now these rivers are many, and mighty, and diverse, and there are four principal ones, of which the greatest and outermost is that called Oceanus, which flows round the earth in a circle; and in the opposite direction flows Acheron, which passes under the earth through desert places, into the Acherusian Lake: this is the lake to the shores of which the souls of the many go when they are dead, and after waiting an appointed time, which is to some a longer and to some a shorter time, they are sent back again to be born as animals. The third river rises between the two, and near the place of rising pours into a vast region of fire, and forms a lake larger than the Mediterranean Sea, boiling with water and mud; and proceeding muddy and turbid, and winding about the earth, comes, among other places, to the extremities of the Acherusian Lake, but mingles not with the waters of the lake, and after making many coils about the earth plunges into Tartarus at a deeper level. This is that Pyriphlegethon, as the stream is called, which throws up jets of fire in all sorts of places. The fourth river goes out on the opposite side, and falls first of all into a wild and savage region, which is all of a dark blue colour, like lapis lazuli; and this is that river which is called the Stygian River, and falls into and forms the Lake Styx, and after falling into the lake and receiving strange powers in the waters, passes under the earth, winding round in the opposite direction to Pyriphlegethon, and meeting in the Acherusian Lake from the opposite side. And the water of this river too mingles with no other, but flows round in a circle and falls into Tartarus over against Pyriphlegethon, and the name of this river, as the poet says, is Cocytus.

'Such is the name of the other world; and when the dead arrive at the place to which the genius of each severally conveys them, first of all they have sentence passed upon them, as they have lived well and piously or not. And those who appear to have lived neither well nor ill, go to the river Acheron, and mount such conveyances as they can get, and are carried in them to the lake, and there they dwell and are purified of their evil deeds, and suffer the penalty of the wrongs which they have done to others, and are absolved, and receive the rewards of their good deeds according to

their deserts. But those who appear to be incurable by reason of the greatness of their crimes – who have committed many and terrible deeds of sacrilege, murders foul and violent, or the like – such are hurled into Tartarus, which is their

suitable destiny, and they never come out. Those again who have committed crimes, which, although great, are not unpardonable – who in a moment of anger, for example, have done violence to a father or mother, and have repented for the remainder of their lives, or who have taken the life of another under like extenuating circumstances – these are plunged into Tartarus, the pains of which they are compelled to undergo for a year, but at the end of the year the wave casts them forth – mere homicides by way of Cocytus, parricides and matricides by Pyriphlegethon – and they are borne to the Acherusian Lake, and there they lift up their voices and call upon the victims whom they have slain or wronged, to have pity on them, and to receive them, and to let them come out of the river into the lake. And if they prevail, then they come forth and cease from their troubles; but if not, they are carried back again into Tartarus and from thence into the rivers unceasingly, until they obtain mercy from those whom they have wronged: for that is the sentence inflicted upon them by their judges. Those also who are remarkable for having led holy lives are released from this earthly prison, and go to their pure home which is above, and dwell in the purer earth; and those who have duly purified themselves with philosophy live henceforth altogether without the body, in mansions fairer far than these, which may not be described, and of which the time would fail me to tell.

'Wherefore, Simmias, seeing all these things, what ought not we to do in order to obtain virtue and wisdom in this life? Fair is the prize, and the hope great.

'I do not mean to affirm that the description which I have given of the soul and her mansions is exactly true – a man of sense ought hardly to say that. But I do say that, inasmuch as the soul is shown to be immortal, he may venture to think, not improperly or unworthily, that something of the kind is true. The venture is a glorious one, and he ought to comfort himself with words like these, which is the reason why lengthen out the tale. Wherefore, I say, let a man be of good cheer about his soul, who has cast away the pleasures and ornaments of the body as alien to him, and rather hurtful in their effects, and has followed after the pleasures of knowledge in this life; who has adorned the soul in her own proper jewels, which are temperance, and justice, and courage, and nobility, and truth – in these arrayed she is ready to go on her journey to the world below, when her time comes. You, Simmias and Cebes, and all other men, will depart at some time or other. Me already, as the tragic poet would say, the voice of fate calls. Soon I must drink the poison; and I think that I had better repair to the bath first, in order that the women may not have the trouble of washing my body after I am dead.'

When he had done speaking, Crito said: 'And have you any commands for us, Socrates – anything to say about your children, or any other matter in which we can serve you?'

'Nothing particular,' he said; 'only, as I have always told you, I would have you look to yourselves; that is a service which you may always be doing to me and mine as well as to yourselves. And you need not make professions; for if you take no thought for yourselves, and walk not according to the precepts which I have given you, not now for the first time, the warmth of your professions will be of no avail.'

'We will do our best,' said Crito. 'But in what way would you have us bury you?'

'In any way that you like; only you must get hold of me, and take care that I do not walk away from you.' Then he turned to us, and added with a smile: 'I cannot make Crito believe that I am the same Socrates who have been talking and conducting the argument; he fancies that I am the other Socrates whom he will soon see, a dead body – and he asks, How shall he bury me? And though I have spoken many words in the endeavour to show that when I have drunk the poison I shall leave you and go to the joys of the blessed – these words of mine, with which I comforted you and myself, have had, I perceive, no effect upon Crito. And therefore I want you to be surety for me now, as he was surety for me at the trial: but let the promise be of another sort; for he was my surety to the judges that I would remain, but you must be my surety to him that I shall not remain, but go away and depart; and then he will suffer less at my death, and not be grieved when he sees my body being burned or buried. I would not have him sorrow at my hard lot, or say at the burial, "Thus we lay out Socrates," or, "Thus we follow him to the grave or bury him;" for false words are not only evil in themselves, but they infect the soul with evil. Be of good cheer, then, my dear Crito, and say that you are burying my body only, and do with that as is usual, and as you think best.'

When he had spoken these words, he arose and went into the bath chamber with Crito, who bade us wait; and we waited, talking and thinking of the subject of discourse, and also of the greatness of our sorrow; he was like a father of whom we were being bereaved, and we were about to pass the rest of our lives as orphans. When he had taken the bath his children were brought to him – (he had two young sons and an elder one); and the women of his family also came, and he talked to them and gave them a few directions in the presence of Crito; and he then dismissed them and returned to us.

Now the hour of sunset was near, for a good deal of time had passed while he was within. When he came out, he sat down with us again after his bath, but not much was said. Soon the jailer, who was the servant of the eleven, entered and stood by him, saying: 'To you, Socrates, whom I know to be the noblest and gentlest and best of all who ever came to this place, I will not impute the angry feelings of other men, who rage and swear at me when, in obedience to the authorities, I bid them drink the poison – indeed, I am sure that you will not be angry with me; for others, as you are aware, and not I, are the guilty cause. And so fare you well, and try to bear lightly what must needs be; you know my errand.' Then bursting into tears he turned away and went out.

Socrates looked at him and said: 'I return your good wishes, and will do as you bid.' Then, turning to us, he said, 'How charming the man is: since I have been in prison he has always been

coming to see me, and at times he would talk to me, and was as good as could be to me, and now see how generously he sorrows for me. But we must do as he says, Crito; let the cup be brought, if the poison is prepared: if not, let the attendant prepare some.'

'Yet,' said Crito, 'the sun is still upon the hilltops, and many a one has taken the draught late, and after the announcement has been made to him, he has eaten and drunk, and indulged in sensual delights; do not hasten then, there is still time.'

Socrates said: 'Yes, Crito, and they of whom you speak are right in doing thus, for they think that they will gain by the delay; but I am right in not doing thus, for I do not think that I should gain anything by drinking the poison a little later; I should be sparing and saving a life which is already gone: I could only laugh at myself for this. Please then to do as I say, and not to refuse me.'

Crito, when he heard this, made a sign to the servant, and the servant went in, and remained for some time, and then returned with the jailer carrying a cup of poison. Socrates said: 'You, my good friend, who are experienced in these matters, shall give me directions how I am to proceed.' The man answered: 'You have only to walk about until your legs are heavy, and then to lie down, and the poison will act.' At the same time he handed the cup to Socrates, who in the easiest and gentlest manner, without the least fear or change of colour or feature, looking at the man with all his eyes, Echecrates, as his manner was, took the cup and said: 'What do you say about making a libation out of this cup to any god? May I, or not?' The man answered: 'We only prepare, Socrates, just so much as we deem enough.' 'I understand,' he said: 'yet I may and must pray to the gods to prosper my journey from this to that other world – may this, then, which is my prayer, be granted to me.' Then holding the cup to his lips, quite readily and cheerfully he drank off the poison. And hitherto most of us had been able to control our sorrow; but now when we saw him drinking, and saw too that he had finished the draught, we could no longer forbear, and in spite of myself my own tears were flowing fast; so that I covered my face

and wept over myself, for certainly I was not weeping over him, but at the thought of my own calamity in having lost such a companion. Nor was I the first, for Crito, when he found himself unable to restrain his tears, had got up and moved away, and I followed; and at that moment, Apollodorus, who had been weeping all the time, broke out in a loud cry which made cowards of us all. Socrates alone retained his calmness: 'What is this strange outcry?' he said. 'I sent away the women mainly in order that they might not offend in this way, for I have heard that a man should die in peace. Be quiet, then, and have patience.'

When we heard that, we were ashamed, and refrained our tears; and he walked about until, as he said, his legs began to fail, and then he lay on his back, according to the directions, and the man who gave him the poison now and then looked at his feet and legs; and after a while he pressed his foot hard and asked him if he could feel; and he said no; and then his leg, and so upwards and upwards, and showed us that he was cold and stiff. And he felt them himself, and said: 'When the poison reaches the heart, that will be the end.' He was beginning to grow cold about the groin, when he uncovered his face, for he had covered himself up, and said (they were his last words) – 'Crito, I owe a cock to Asclepius; will you remember to pay the debt?' 'The debt shall be paid,' said Crito; 'is there anything else?' There was no answer to this question; but in a minute or two a movement was heard, and the attendants uncovered him; his eyes were set, and Crito closed his eyes and mouth.

Such was the end, Echecrates, of our friend, whom I may truly call the wisest, and justest, and best of all the men whom I have ever known.

THE END